C++ Networking 101

Unlocking Sockets, Protocols, VPNs, and Asynchronous I/O with 75+ sample programs

Anais Sutherland

Published by: GitforGits
Publisher: Sonal Dhandre
www.gitforgits.com
support@gitforgits.com

Printed in India

First Printing: May 2023

ISBN: 978-8119177127

Cover Design by: Kitten Publishing

Content

Preface xii

Prologue xvi

CHAPTER 1: INTRODUCTION TO NETWORKING AND C++ **1**

Understanding C++ for Networking 2

Refreshing C++ Basics 3

Basic Syntax 3

Data Types 3

Variables 4

Constants 4

Operators 5

Control Structures 5

Arrays 5

Strings 5

Pointers 6

Functions 6

Data Structures 6

C++ Libraries for Networking 7

Boost.Asio 7

POCO C++ Libraries 8

cURLpp 8

Setting up C++ Environment 9

Install C++ Compiler 9

Install IDE 10

Install Networking Libraries 10

cURLpp 11

Summary 12

CHAPTER 2: UNDERSTANDING INTERNET PROTOCOLS - TCP AND UDP **14**

Exploring Internet Protocols 15
Deep into Transmission Control Protocol (TCP) 16
Basic Structure of TCP 16
TCP Handshake and Connection 17
TCP Data Transfer 17
TCP Connection Termination 18
Deep Dive into User Datagram Protocol (UDP) 18
Basic Structure of UDP 18
UDP Operation 19
UDP Data Transfer 19
Error Checking and Recovery 19
Comparing TCP and UDP – When to use Which? 20
Connection Orientation 20
Reliability 20
Flow Control and Congestion Control 20
Speed 21
When to use TCP or UDP 21
Use TCP when 21
Use UDP when 21
Sockets and Socket Programming 22
What is a Socket? 22
Socket Programming in C++ 22
TCP Client-Server Socket Programming 23
Setting up Boost.Asio 23
Server Application 23
Client Application 25
UDP Client-Server Socket Programming 26
Server Application 26
Client Application 28
Socket Programming Best Practices 29

Summary ... 30

CHAPTER 3: NETWORK INTERFACES AND ADDRESSING ... **32**

Overview of Network Interfaces and Addressing ... 33

Understanding Network Interfaces ... 34

Network Interfaces in Windows ... 34

Network Interfaces in Linux ... 34

IP Addresses and Subnets ... 35

IP Addresses ... 35

Subnets ... 35

Perform Subnetting and IP Configuration ... 36

Install Boost and ASIO ... 36

Retrieve IP Address ... 36

Working with IP Addresses ... 37

Create TCP Server and Client ... 37

Creating a Simple TCP Server ... 38

Creating a Simple TCP Client ... 39

Common Challenges in TCP/UDP Connections ... 40

Summary ... 41

CHAPTER 4: APPLICATION LAYER PROTOCOLS ... **43**

Application Layer ... 44

HTTP (HyperText Transfer Protocol) ... 44

HTTPS (HyperText Transfer Protocol Secure) ... 45

FTP (File Transfer Protocol) ... 45

SMTP (Simple Mail Transfer Protocol) ... 46

IMAP (Internet Message Access Protocol) ... 46

DNS (Domain Name System) ... 46

HTTP and HTTPS Deep Dive ... 47

Send HTTP Request using Boost Beast ... 47

Using Boost Asio SSL for HTTPS request ... 49

FTP Deep Dive ... 52

Implement FTP using Curl 52
SMTP & IMAP Deep Dive 54
Send Email using Vmime Library 54
Receive Emails using VMime 55
DNS Deep Dive 57
Types of DNS Queries 58
Perform DNS Query using Boost ASIO 58
Error Handling in Socket Programming 59
Summary 60
CHAPTER 5: VPNS **62**
Introduction to Virtual Private Networks 63
Overview 63
Components of VPN 63
Applications of VPN 64
Types of VPN 65
Site-to-Site VPN 65
Remote Access VPN 66
VPN Protocols 66
Types of VPN Protocols 67
Explore OpenVPN 67
Setting up OpenVPN 68
Implementing Site-to-Site VPN 69
Implementing Remote Access VPN 70
Summary 72
CHAPTER 6: WIRELESS NETWORKS **74**
Introduction to Wireless Networks 75
Wireless Fidelity (WiFi) 75
WiFi Programming using C++ 76
Bluetooth 77
Bluetooth Programming with BlueZ 79

Zigbee 81

Zigbee Programming using C++ 81

Wireless Standards: 802.11a/b/g/n/ac/ax 83

802.11a 83

802.11b 83

802.11g 84

802.11n (Wi-Fi 4) 84

802.11ac (Wi-Fi 5) 84

802.11ax (Wi-Fi 6) 84

Wireless Security Standards 85

Wired Equivalent Privacy (WEP) 86

Wi-Fi Protected Access (WPA) 86

WPA2 86

WPA3 87

General Practices for Programming Wireless Networks 88

Scan Available Networks 88

Connecting to Network 89

Error Handling 89

Sample Program on Querying Wireless Connection 90

Summary 91

CHAPTER 7: ASYNCHRONOUS PROGRAMMING 93

Getting Started with Asynchronous Programming 94

What is Asynchronous Programming? 94

Why not Synchronous Programming? 94

Callbacks, Promises, and Async/Await 95

Callbacks 95

Futures and Promises 96

Async/Await 97

Writing Asynchronous using Callbacks 98

Multithreading and Concurrency 101

Exploring Multithreading ... 101
Understanding Concurrency ... 101
Creating Multi-threaded Server ... 102
Asynchronous I/O and libuv ... 104
What is Asynchronous I/O? ... 104
Explore Libuv ... 104
Sample Program on Asynchronous I/O ... 105
Sample Program on TCP Echo Server using libuv ... 109
Summary ... 111
CHAPTER 8: NETWORK TESTING AND SIMULATION ... 113
Overview ... 114
Network Testing Methodologies ... 114
Functional Testing ... 115
Step-by-Step ... 116
Conduct Functional Testing using PcapPlus ... 117
Performance Testing ... 118
Step-by-Step ... 118
Conduct Performance Testing on TCP Server ... 120
Stress Testing ... 121
Perform Network Stress Testing ... 121
Security Testing ... 122
Using ARP for Security Testing ... 123
Network Simulations ... 124
Overview ... 124
Benefits ... 124
Performing Network Simulations ... 125
NS-3 ... 127
Features of NS-3 ... 127
Network Simulation using NS-3 ... 128
Process of Network Simulation ... 128

Setting up Network Simulation using NS-3 129
Summary 132
CHAPTER 9: NETWORK CONFIGURATION MANAGEMENT **133**
Network Configurations Overview 134
Network Configuration Protocol (NETCONF) 135
What is NETCONF? 135
NETCONF Message 135
NETCONF using C++ 136
NETCONF Process 136
Various Network Configuration Tasks 138
Device Configuration 138
Security Configuration 138
Performance Tuning 139
Diagnostics and Monitoring 139
Fault Management and Recovery 139
Software and Firmware Updates 139
Protocol Configuration 139
Configuration via NETCONF 139
Automating Firmware Updates 140
Manipulate Settings of TCP and UDP 142
Recovery during Failure 144
Store Configuration 144
Read Configuration 144
Apply Configuration 145
Recover from Failure 145
Automate Running Diagnostic Tools 145
Configure Access Control Lists and Firewalls 146
Summary 147
CHAPTER 10: NETWORK MONITORING **149**
Network Monitoring Overview 150

Fault Monitoring 150
Understanding Nagios 151
Install and Configure Nagios 151
Monitor Hosts and Services on Nagios 154
Using Nagios for Fault Monitoring 156
Sample Program to Perform Fault Monitoring 157
Performance Monitoring 158
Using Nagios for Performance Monitoring 159
Security Monitoring 160
Perform Security Monitoring using Nagios 162
Account Monitoring 164
Perform Account Monitoring with Custom Nagios Plugin 165
Summary 166
CHAPTER 11: NETWORK TROUBLESHOOTING 168
Beginning with Network Troubleshooting 169
Network Troubleshooting Methodology 169
Identify 170
Diagnose 170
Propose 170
Test 170
Document 170
Using Ping 171
Example 1: Basic Ping 171
Example 2: Limit Number of Ping Requests 171
Example 3: Increasing the Timeout 172
Using Tracert/Traceroute 172
Example 1: Basic Traceroute 173
Example 2: Specifying the Number of Hops 173
Example 3: Using ICMP instead of UDP 173
Using Nslookup 174

Example 1: Basic Nslookup 174
Example 2: Reverse DNS Lookup 174
Example 3: Querying Specific DNS Record Type 174
Using Netstat 174
Example 1: Basic Netstat 175
Example 2: Displaying Only Listening Sockets 175
Example 3: Displaying Statistics 175
Example 4: Continuously Display Network Status 175
Exploring Wireshark 175
About Wireshark 175
Features 176
Installation of Wireshark 176
Wireshark Configuration 176
Exploring Tcpdump 177
About Tcpdump 177
Features 177
Installation of Tcpdump 177
Examples 178
Summary 179
Index 182
Epilogue 184

Preface

This book is an invaluable resource for aspiring network administrators aiming to deepen their understanding of networking concepts while strengthening their C++ programming skills. Across eleven chapters, this book bridges the gap between network administration and programming, providing readers a holistic approach to mastering network operations. Readers begin with a deep-dive into network fundamentals such as TCP/IP model, sockets, and protocols. They then progress to practical programming, employing C++ to establish TCP/UDP client-server connections, handle network errors, and deal with application layer protocols such as HTTP/HTTPS, FTP, SMTP, IMAP, and DNS.

The book then guides readers through Virtual Private Networks (VPNs), detailing their importance, functioning, and the distinct types of VPNs. It explores wireless networking and asynchronous programming, providing clear illustrations of WiFi, Bluetooth, Zigbee setup using C++. It covers critical wireless standards and security protocols. For a comprehensive understanding, the book illustrates network configuration management using C++ to automate crucial network operations tasks, thus highlighting the power of programming in network management.

Advanced topics include network testing and simulations, which provide insights into performance enhancement and network robustness. A detailed exploration of network monitoring enhances the reader's skillset, teaching ways to conduct fault, performance, security, and account monitoring. In the end, the book rounds up with network troubleshooting, elucidating several essential network troubleshooting tools and methodologies.

In this book you will learn how to:

- Understand TCP/IP model and protocols with hands-on C++ programming.
- Master TCP/UDP client-server connections and error handling.
- Grasp application layer protocols like HTTP/HTTPS, FTP, SMTP, IMAP, and DNS.
- Discover the importance and use of VPNs and how to set them up.
- Learn about wireless networking and asynchronous programming.
- Gain insights into network configuration management.
- Understand network testing methodologies and simulations.
- Learn to monitor various aspects of a network using Nagios.
- Learn about essential network troubleshooting tools and methodologies.

- Enhance network performance and reliability through C++ programming.

The essence of this book lies in its practical approach. With ample illustrations, code snippets, and hands-on exercises using C++, this book stands out as a definitive guide for anyone aiming to become a competent network administrator, equipped with the power of programming.

GitforGits

Prerequisites

This book is suitable for every computer programmer or computer science graduate with a basic understanding of C++. No prior networking knowledge is required. A familiarity with fundamental C++ concepts, such as variables, loops, and basic syntax, is assumed. By focusing on practical examples and clear explanations, this guide ensures a fast-paced learning experience.

Codes Usage

Are you in need of some helpful code examples to assist you in your programming and documentation? Look no further! Our book offers a wealth of supplemental material, including code examples and exercises.

Not only is this book here to aid you in getting your job done, but you have our permission to use the example code in your programs and documentation. However, please note that if you are reproducing a significant portion of the code, we do require you to contact us for permission.

But don't worry, using several chunks of code from this book in your program or answering a question by citing our book and quoting example code does not require permission. But if you do choose to give credit, an attribution typically includes the title, author, publisher, and ISBN. For example, "C++ Networking 101 by Anais Sutherland".

If you are unsure whether your intended use of the code examples falls under fair use or the permissions outlined above, please do not hesitate to reach out to us at support@gitforgits.com.

We are happy to assist and clarify any concerns.

Acknowledgement

I owe a tremendous debt of gratitude to GitforGits, for their unflagging enthusiasm and wise counsel throughout the entire process of writing this book. Their knowledge and careful editing helped make sure the piece was useful for people of all reading levels and comprehension skills. In addition, I'd like to thank everyone involved in the publishing process for their efforts in making this book a reality. Their efforts, from copyediting to advertising, made the project what it is today.

Finally, I'd like to express my gratitude to everyone who has shown me unconditional love and encouragement throughout my life. Their support was crucial to the completion of this book. I appreciate your help with this endeavour and your continued interest in my career.

Prologue

There is a force at work in the vastness of the digital universe that makes it possible to navigate with ease, remain connected at all times, and have confidential conversations. The network is the driving force behind modern digital communication and serves as its fulcrum. Because the world will continue to rely heavily on digital interaction in the foreseeable future, there will be an ever-increasing demand for highly trained individuals to serve as administrators of computer networks. However, there is a disparity between the growing demand for skilled network administrators and the available supply of those administrators. This void is something that the author of "C++ Networking 101" hopes to fill.

The initiative known as "C++ Networking 101" is more than just a book; it is an effort to train a new generation of network administrators who are prepared to meet the challenges of digital communication both now and in the foreseeable future. This book is organized in such a way that it will gradually teach the reader the knowledge and practical skills that are necessary for the job. Aspiring network administrators will benefit from reading this book because it will help them gain a comprehensive understanding of various networking concepts while also improving their C++ programming abilities. First, we cover the fundamentals of networks, including protocols and the TCP/IP model. Then, we gradually progress to more advanced topics, including virtual private networks (VPNs), wireless networking, asynchronous programming, network configuration management, and network testing.

Each chapter has been meticulously crafted to ensure that you understand the networking topic at hand, see its implementation in C++, and finally witness its practical demonstration. This has been done in order to provide you with the best possible learning experience. Real-life examples and in-depth case studies inject excitement and relevance into the educational process. When you have finished reading this book, you will not only have an understanding of the responsibilities of a network administrator, but you will also have the skills necessary to perform these responsibilities using C++.

I want to encourage you to go on this journey with me so that you can discover the fascinating world of networking. Deciphering the complexities of network administration using the power of C++ will allow us to uncover the path to becoming skilled network administrators. Let's begin our journey!

Chapter 1: Introduction to Networking and C++

Understanding C++ for Networking

C++, developed by Bjarne Stroustrup in 1985, is a general-purpose programming language that has become a cornerstone in the world of programming. Designed as an extension of the C language, C++ introduced the concept of classes and objects, heralding a new era of Object-Oriented Programming (OOP). C++ is celebrated for its efficiency and control; its performance is comparable to lower-level languages like C, while it also offers high-level abstraction.

Fundamentally, C++ provides a robust platform for various software development needs, including system software, game development, web servers, and notably, for our purposes, network programming. Its use in the latter stems from several key features. The language is highly portable, making it possible to write a program on one platform and run it on another with little or no modification. Its performance is fast and efficient, which is critical when managing complex networking tasks that require real-time responses. Lastly, the rich library support of C++ offers a plethora of tools and functionalities, making it a popular choice for network engineers and administrators. C++ has been instrumental in network programming for decades. The primary reason for this is its ability to provide direct control over the system hardware. This means that network administrators can control network interfaces, packets, and even implement protocols using the language. This kind of control is paramount in a field where performance and security can never be compromised.

In the world of networking, C++ is widely used to develop network devices and protocols, network simulations, packet crafting, and network analysis tools, to name a few applications. One of the main reasons network administrators and engineers favour C++ is its ability to interact with the underlying operating system through system-level programming. This is particularly beneficial in network programming, as it allows developers to manipulate network resources and configurations efficiently. C++ also boasts of several networking libraries that make the task of networking more streamlined and manageable. Libraries such as Boost.Asio, POCO C++, and ACE (Adaptive Communication Environment) provide an extensive, flexible, and portable interface for programming network applications. These libraries cater to everything from lower-level network programming, such as managing sockets and handling protocols, to higher-level tasks like creating and managing servers. For network administrators, these libraries can reduce the complexity of their tasks and increase the performance of their systems.

Moreover, the growth of modern C++ standards has introduced many enhancements that have made C++ more user-friendly, efficient, and safer. Concepts such as smart pointers and lambda expressions have made C++ code cleaner and more maintainable. For network administrators, this is a significant advantage as it allows them to write networking code that is easier to understand, test, and debug. C++ has a significant role in network programming due to its combination of performance, control, system-level access, and rich library support. As the networking landscape continues to evolve, so does the functionality and capabilities of C++, solidifying its position in the toolkit of any proficient network administrator. This book aims to take you on a journey through the world of networking using C++, offering both the theory behind the concepts and practical examples to cement your understanding. By the end of this journey, you will be well equipped to tackle the challenges of network administration using C++ as your primary tool. Let us begin this exciting journey.

Refreshing C++ Basics

As you embark on your journey to master C++ for network administration, it's crucial to have a firm grasp on the fundamentals of the language. Although you have prior knowledge, refreshing these concepts can provide a stronger foundation for the more complex topics ahead. Let us dive into the syntax and data structures in C++. C++ is a statically typed, compiled, general-purpose, case-sensitive, free-form programming language. A C++ program generally consists of one or more functions, one of which must be named main(). The main function serves as the starting point for program execution.

Basic Syntax

In the C++ programming language, a statement is terminated with a semicolon (;). Code blocks, typically used for function bodies, loops, and conditionals, are enclosed within curly braces {}. Comments can be added using either double slashes (//) for single-line comments or forward slash followed by an asterisk (/) and ending with an asterisk followed by a forward slash (/) for multi-line comments.

A simple C++ statement might look like this:

```
int a = 10; // This is a single line comment
```

Data Types

C++ supports several types of data:

- Integer types: Represent numbers without a decimal point. They are further divided into short, int, long, and long long, with varying sizes and ranges. Signed and unsigned versions are available for each type, with unsigned types unable to represent negative numbers.

- Floating-Point types: Represent numbers with a decimal point. They come in float, double, and long double varieties, each with different precision levels and ranges.
- Boolean type: Represent true or false values.
- Character types: Represent single characters.
- Void type: Represents the absence of value.

```
int num = 10;
double pi = 3.14159;
bool is_true = true;
char initial = 'A';
```

Variables

A variable provides us with named storage that our programs can manipulate. Variables in C++ are typed. When you declare a variable, you must specify its type, which determines the size and layout of the variable's memory, the range of values it can hold, and the set of operations that can be applied to it.

```
int age;
double average;
char initial;
```

Constants

Constants, in the context of programming, refer to values that remain fixed and unchangeable throughout the execution of a program. Literals, on the other hand, are a subset of constants that are directly used to express specific values within the source code. Examples of literals are numerical values, characters enclosed in single quotes, and strings enclosed in double quotes. They serve as static representations of certain data types, providing an intuitive way to input and manipulate data in programming.

```
#define PI 3.14159 // symbolic constant
const int max_age = 150; // const keyword
```

Operators

C++ offers a comprehensive set of operators, supporting a wide range of programming needs. This includes arithmetic operators such as addition (+), subtraction (-), multiplication (*), division (/), and modulo (%), used for performing basic mathematical operations. Comparison operators like equal to (==), not equal to (!=), greater than (>), less than (<), greater than or equal to (>=), and less than or equal to (<=) enable comparisons between variables. Logical operators include and (&&), or (| |), and not (!), providing the foundation for logic-based decision-making. Lastly, C++ supports bitwise operators such as and (&), or (|), xor (^), not (~), left shift (<<), and right shift (>>), allowing for direct manipulation of binary data.

Control Structures

Control structures are fundamental components in programming that modify the path or flow of execution. They come in different types, including conditional and iterative. Conditional structures like 'if', 'if-else', and 'switch' allow for decisions to be made based on certain conditions. For instance, 'if' executes a block of code if a specified condition is true. Conversely, iterative structures like 'for', 'while', and 'do-while' facilitate repetitive execution of code blocks, making them ideal for looping tasks. Understanding and applying these control structures effectively is crucial for efficient and functional programming.

Arrays

An array is a powerful data structure, adept at storing a fixed-size sequential collection of homogeneous elements. This means it can hold a certain number of values, all of the same data type, arranged in a strict sequence. Consider an array as an organized collection of same-type variables. For example,

```
int arr[5] = {10, 20, 30, 40, 50};
```

'arr' stores five integers. Each element can be individually accessed, making arrays ideal for data manipulation and computational algorithms.

Strings

In C++, strings can be expressed in two primary ways. Firstly, they can be represented as an array of characters, an older method inherited from the C language.

```
char str1[] = "Hello";
```

```
string str2 = "World";
```

This entails declaring a char array, for example, char str1[] = "Hello";, where str1 is an array that stores the string "Hello". Secondly, C++ introduced a more versatile string class. A string can be declared like so: string str2 = "World";. In this case, str2 is a string object storing "World". Both methods have their unique applications in programming.

Pointers

A pointer is a specialized type of variable designed to store a memory address, typically indicating the position of another variable within the computer's memory. This core feature provides a foundation for dynamic memory allocation and manipulation, enabling developers to create, manage, and modify data structures, including linked lists and trees. The flexibility and efficiency offered by pointers are instrumental for implementing advanced algorithms and handling complex data structures in many programming paradigms, especially in languages like C and C++.

```
int var = 20;
int *p = &var;
```

Functions

A function in programming is essentially a block of code composed of various statements to accomplish a specific task. In the C++ programming language, each program must contain at least one function, typically named 'main()'. This function serves as the entry point of the program and orchestrates the execution of other functions if present. Beyond the main(), even the most straightforward C++ programs may define and use additional functions to simplify code, enhance readability, and facilitate code reuse.

```
void greet() {
 cout << "Hello, World!";
}
```

Data Structures

C++ includes several advanced data structures as part of its Standard Template Library (STL), including Vector (dynamic arrays), List (doubly linked list), Stack, Queue, Priority_queue, Set, Map (associative array), etc. These data structures are templated, so they can be used with any valid data type.

```
std::vector<int> nums = {1, 2, 3, 4, 5};
std::map<string, int> ages = {{"Alice", 25}, {"Bob", 30}};
```

From simple scripts to complex systems, these basic concepts form the foundation for all C++ programming tasks, including those in network administration. By mastering these concepts, you are well on your way to harnessing the full power of C++ in networking.

C++ Libraries for Networking

As we delve further into the realms of C++ networking, it's essential to familiarize ourselves with some crucial libraries that will be our primary tools for the job. C++ comes equipped with a plethora of libraries, each designed to address different aspects of networking. However, for the sake of brevity and focus, we will concentrate on three libraries that are popular and widely preferred by network professionals: Boost.Asio, POCO C++, and cURLpp.

Boost.Asio

Boost.Asio is a cross-platform C++ library used for network and low-level I/O programming. It provides developers with a consistent and efficient model for asynchronous programming, which is incredibly beneficial for networking applications that often involve waiting for responses from a network.

Key Features

- Asynchronous Programming Model: Boost.Asio offers asynchronous operations for networking, timers, serial I/O, and more. This allows for high performance and scalability in network applications, as it reduces the time wasted while waiting for network responses.
- Support for IPv4 and IPv6: Boost.Asio supports both IPv4 and IPv6 protocols. As more networks are transitioning to IPv6, this feature is highly beneficial.
- SSL Support: Boost.Asio provides support for the SSL (Secure Sockets Layer) protocol, ensuring secure communication over the network.
- Timer Support: It offers timer functionality, allowing you to schedule and handle operations after a certain time period.
- Multithreading Support: Boost.Asio can run handlers in multiple threads, which makes it suitable for multi-core processors.

POCO C++ Libraries

POCO C++ Libraries, standing for POrtable COmponents, are a collection of open-source C++ class libraries that simplify and accelerate the development of network-centric applications. POCO is excellent for producing modular and efficient code and is especially useful for systems that need to be portable across different platforms.

Key Features

- Platform Independence: POCO C++ libraries are highly portable and can be compiled and run on multiple platforms.
- Network Protocols: POCO supports a wide range of network protocols, including HTTP, FTP, SMTP, POP3, and more. It also provides support for handling URIs and HTTP-based web services.
- Database Access: It offers classes for database access, which is beneficial for network applications that need to interact with databases.
- File System Access: POCO provides classes for handling files, directories, and paths in a platform-independent way.
- Multithreading and Synchronization: POCO offers powerful multithreading capabilities and synchronization classes like Mutex, Semaphore, Event, etc.

cURLpp

cURLpp is a C++ wrapper for libcURL. cURL is a command-line tool for transferring data using various network protocols, and cURLpp brings this power and flexibility to C++ applications. This library is widely used for HTTP requests, which form a significant part of modern network administration tasks.

Key Features

- Multiple Protocol Support: cURLpp supports a wide array of protocols, including HTTP, HTTPS, FTP, FTPS, SCP, SFTP, TFTP, LDAP, and more.
- SSL and TLS Support: It supports secure communication using SSL and TLS protocols.
- Cookie Handling: cURLpp provides functionalities for handling HTTP cookies, useful for web-based network applications.
- File Transfer: cURLpp can be used to transfer files to and from servers using the supported protocols.
- HTTP POST and Form Uploads: It supports HTTP POST operations and multipart form uploads.

The above libraries make your journey into C++ networking more efficient and manageable. Each library offers its unique capabilities, and understanding when and how to utilize them is key to becoming a proficient network administrator with C++. In the upcoming chapters, we'll delve deeper into each of these libraries and explore their functionalities with hands-on examples and exercises.

Setting up C++ Environment

Establishing your C++ programming environment involves a series of vital steps. You'll need to install a C++ compiler, such as GCC or Clang, for translating your code. Also, installing an Integrated Development Environment (IDE) like Visual Studio or Code::Blocks is essential for efficient coding. Lastly, download and set up libraries that you'll utilize in your projects. These may range from standard libraries to more specialized ones, depending on the nature of your work.

Below is how to do it:

Install C++ Compiler

The first thing you need is a C++ compiler. We'll use MinGW (Minimalist GNU for Windows), which is a port of the popular GCC compiler for Windows.

Visit the MinGW project's website.

Click the "Download" button or go directly to the download page.

Download the MinGW installer (mingw-get-setup.exe).

Run the installer and choose your settings. You can install MinGW to any directory, but for simplicity, we recommend C:\MinGW.

In the installer, choose the basic setup on the left and mark mingw32-base for installation.

Apply the changes and wait for the installation to finish.

After installation, add C:\MinGW\bin to your PATH environment variable.

Press Win + X and choose "System".

Click "Advanced system settings".

In the "System Properties" window, click "Environment Variables".

In "System variables", find and select "Path", then click "Edit".

Click "New" and add C:\MinGW\bin.

You can test the installation by opening a new command prompt and typing g++ --version. It should print the installed version of GCC.

Install IDE

Next, you'll need an Integrated Development Environment (IDE). An IDE helps you write and organize your code, and it often comes with features like code completion, debugging tools, and more. For C++, we recommend Visual Studio Code (VS Code).

Go to the VS Code download page.

Download the installer for Windows.

Run the installer, accept the agreement, and click "Next" until the installation starts.

Open VS Code after the installation is complete.

You'll also need to install the C++ extension for VS Code.

Open VS Code and click on the Extensions view icon on the Sidebar (or press Ctrl+Shift+X).

Search for 'c++'.

Click Install on the "C/C++" extension provided by Microsoft.

Install Networking Libraries

Finally, let us install the networking libraries.

Boost.Asio

Download the latest version of Boost from the official website.

Extract the downloaded file to a directory, e.g., C:\boost.

Open a command prompt in the directory where you extracted Boost and run these commands:

```
bootstrap.bat
.\b2.exe
```

This will build and install Boost, which may take a while. After it's done, add C:\boost\boost_1_xx_0 to your include path and C:\boost\boost_1_xx_0\stage\lib to your library path.

POCO C++

Download the latest POCO C++ Libraries from the official website.

Extract the downloaded file to a directory, e.g., C:\poco.

Open a command prompt in the directory where you extracted POCO and run these commands:

```
buildwin.cmd 141
```

Replace 141 with your Visual Studio version number.

This will build POCO. After it's done, add C:\poco\include to your include path and C:\poco\lib to your library path.

cURLpp

cURLpp is a wrapper for libcURL, so you need to install libcURL first.

Download the latest version of libcURL from the official website.

Extract the downloaded file to a directory, e.g., C:\curl.

Open a command prompt in the directory where you extracted libcURL and run these commands:

```
buildconf.bat
nmake /f Makefile.vc mode=dll VC=15
```

Replace 15 with your Visual Studio version number.

This will build libcURL. After it's done, add C:\curl\include to your include path and C:\curl\lib to your library path.

Then, download the latest version of cURLpp from the official GitHub.

Extract the downloaded file to a directory, e.g., C:\curlpp.

Open a command prompt in the directory where you extracted cURLpp and run these commands:

```
cmake . -G "Visual Studio 15 2017" -DCURLPP_BUILD_EXAMPLES=OFF -
DCURLPP_BUILD_TESTS=OFF
```

Replace "Visual Studio 15 2017" with your version of Visual Studio.

This will generate a Visual Studio solution file. Open this file in Visual Studio and build the solution.

After it's done, add C:\curlpp\include to your include path and C:\curlpp\lib to your library path.

Now, you're all set to explore the exciting world of C++ networking!

Summary

In this chapter, we walked through the initial setup of your C++ environment on a Windows platform, paving the way for a hands-on exploration of network programming in C++. The journey began with the installation of MinGW, a GCC compiler port that enables C++ development on Windows. We also discussed how to adjust the system's PATH variable to recognize the compiler, a crucial step that often poses challenges for beginners.

Following this, we delved into setting up Visual Studio Code, an advanced and yet user-friendly Integrated Development Environment (IDE) preferred by many C++ developers. With Visual Studio Code, writing and organizing your code becomes considerably easier, thanks to its features such as syntax highlighting, auto code completion, and an integrated terminal. Furthermore, we demonstrated how to enhance Visual Studio Code's capabilities by adding the C++ extension, a move that provides added support for C++ development.

Finally, we installed and set up three influential C++ networking libraries—Boost.Asio,

POCO C++, and cURLpp. Each library comes with a unique set of features that address various aspects of network programming. Understanding these libraries and knowing how to install them is fundamental for any network professional. By the end of this chapter, you should have a fully operational C++ development environment on your Windows machine, complete with the primary tools you'll need as we delve deeper into network programming using C++.

CHAPTER 2: UNDERSTANDING INTERNET PROTOCOLS - TCP AND UDP

Exploring Internet Protocols

Internet protocols form the backbone of networking, acting as the rules and conventions that govern the interaction between devices over a network. These protocols ensure smooth communication by defining the precise format and order of messages exchanged between systems and the actions taken on message transmission and receipt.

Understanding these protocols is akin to learning the language of networking; only by mastering this language can one communicate effectively with networked devices and services. In this chapter, we'll delve into the world of internet protocols, exploring their utility in today's modern networking scenario and understanding their immense popularity among network administrators. To understand the utility of internet protocols, consider the analogy of a postal system. When you post a letter, it has to go through various stages—collection, sorting, transportation, and delivery. Each stage is governed by rules or "protocols" that ensure the letter reaches its intended recipient correctly. Similarly, internet protocols govern the journey of data packets across the internet—from their formation at the source to their receipt at the destination.

In the current era, where everything is interconnected—from computers, smartphones, and tablets to IoT devices, smart home devices, and industrial machinery—the importance of internet protocols has increased manifold. These protocols ensure that data is transmitted securely, reliably, and efficiently across networks, whether it's a video call, an email, a web page, or sensor data from an IoT device. Internet protocols are also critical in ensuring interoperability. As the internet brings together a multitude of devices from different manufacturers running on different operating systems, the protocols act as a universal language that all these devices understand and adhere to. This guarantees that any device can communicate with any other, regardless of their make or model.

Among the many internet protocols, some are more popular due to their widespread use and versatility. For example, the TCP/IP protocol suite, which includes protocols like TCP, IP, UDP, HTTP, and many others, is the foundation of the modern internet. TCP/IP ensures that data packets are routed correctly from source to destination, with TCP providing reliable, ordered, and error-checked delivery of a stream of bytes. Another popular protocol is HTTP, used by web browsers to fetch web pages from servers. Its secure version, HTTPS, ensures that the communication between the browser and the server is encrypted and secure from eavesdropping.

In the realm of email, protocols like SMTP, IMAP, and POP3 are popular. SMTP is used for sending emails, while IMAP and POP3 are used for receiving them. Each has its benefits and is chosen based on the specific requirements of the email service. In the world of IoT, protocols like MQTT and CoAP have gained popularity due to their lightweight nature, making them suitable for devices with limited resources.

Internet protocols are the heart of networking, enabling seamless and effective communication between devices. Their utility in today's interconnected world cannot be overstated, and they are a vital part of any network administrator's toolkit. Understanding these protocols is not just a requirement, but a necessity for anyone aspiring to excel in the field of networking. As we progress further, we will explore these protocols in more detail, focusing on their usage in network programming with C++.

Deep into Transmission Control Protocol (TCP)

The Transmission Control Protocol (TCP) is one of the fundamental protocols of the internet, providing reliable, ordered, and error-checked delivery of a stream of bytes. It is a part of the TCP/IP protocol suite and operates at the transport layer. Let us dive into the aspects of TCP in detail.

Basic Structure of TCP

In TCP, data is transmitted in the form of packets, specifically called "segments". Each TCP segment contains a header and data. The header, which is 20 to 60 bytes long, contains information needed for the proper delivery of data, including source and destination port numbers, sequence number, acknowledgement number, data offset, reserved, control flags, window, checksum, and urgent pointer as below:

1) Source and Destination Port Numbers: These are 16-bit fields that identify the ports on the source and destination machines.

2) Sequence Number: This 32-bit field represents the number assigned to the first byte of data in the current message.

3) Acknowledgement Number: Also 32-bits, this field indicates the value of the next sequence number that the sender of the segment is expecting to receive.

4) Data Offset: This field indicates where the data begins in the segment.

5) Control Flags: These are used to control the flow of data. They include SYN, ACK, FIN, RST, PSH, and URG flags.

6) Window: This field specifies the size of the sender's receive window (the buffer

space available for incoming data).

7) Checksum: This is used for error-checking of the header and data.

8) Urgent Pointer: When the URG flag is set, this field points to the sequence number of the byte following the urgent data.

TCP Handshake and Connection

Before any data transfer can occur between two devices using TCP, a connection must be established. This is done using a process known as the "three-way handshake". The purpose of the handshake is to synchronize the sequence and acknowledgment numbers of both sender and receiver, and to exchange TCP window sizes as below:

1) SYN: The initiating device sends a SYN segment to the server, with an arbitrary sequence number (let's call it X).

2) SYN-ACK: Upon receiving the SYN, the server responds with a SYN-ACK segment. The acknowledgement number is set to X+1, and the sequence number is another arbitrary number (let's call it Y).

3) ACK: Finally, the initiating device sends an ACK segment back to the server with the acknowledgment number set to Y+1. This completes the handshake, and the connection is established.

TCP Data Transfer

When a connection is initiated between two computing systems, it enables the process of data transfer. This connection, established over a network, facilitates the movement of data packets from one system to another. Each segment or piece of data dispatched is labeled with a distinct sequence number, serving as an identifier for tracking and maintaining the order of transmission. The receiving system, upon successfully acquiring a data segment, dispatches an acknowledgment signal back to the sender. This acknowledgment confirms the reception of the specific data segment, thus ensuring the integrity and accuracy of the data transfer. This iterative process of sending, acknowledging, and confirming creates a reliable and effective communication protocol, vital for ensuring efficient and error-free data transfers.

TCP Connection Termination

The termination of a TCP connection involves another handshake process:

1) FIN: When a device is ready to end the connection, it sends a FIN segment, indicating that it has no more data to send.

2) ACK: Upon receiving the FIN, the other device sends an ACK for the FIN. At this point, the connection is half-closed.

3) FIN: Eventually, when the other device is also ready to end the connection, it sends its own FIN.

4) ACK: The first device sends an ACK for the received FIN, and the connection is fully closed.

Understanding the intricacies of TCP is vital for any network administrator or network programmer, as it forms the backbone of many internet communications. When writing network programs in C++, knowing the inner workings of TCP allows for the creation of reliable and efficient applications

Deep Dive into User Datagram Protocol (UDP)

The User Datagram Protocol (UDP) is another crucial protocol in the TCP/IP suite, operating alongside TCP at the transport layer. However, unlike TCP, which is connection-oriented and reliable, UDP is connectionless and does not guarantee delivery of data. This makes it simpler and faster than TCP, which is advantageous in certain scenarios. Let us explore the details of UDP.

Basic Structure of UDP

Like TCP, UDP also transmits data in packets, known as "datagrams". Each UDP datagram comprises a header and data. The header is much simpler than a TCP header, consisting of only four fields each of 16 bits - source port, destination port, length, and checksum as below:

1) Source and Destination Port Numbers: These identify the sending and receiving applications.

2) Length: This field specifies the length of the entire datagram (header and data).

3) Checksum: This is used for error-checking of the header and data. It's optional in IPv4 but mandatory in IPv6.

UDP Operation

Given its connectionless nature, UDP doesn't require a handshake to establish a connection before data transfer. Instead, a device can start sending datagrams to another device as long as it knows the IP address and port number. Each datagram is independent of others – hence UDP is often referred to as an "unreliable" protocol.

UDP Data Transfer

During data transfer, each UDP datagram is sent independently and can arrive at the destination in any order. Unlike TCP, UDP doesn't provide sequence numbers to order the received datagrams. If ordering is required, it must be managed by the application layer.

Furthermore, UDP does not provide flow control or congestion control. There's no mechanism to manage the rate of data sent or to adjust it based on network congestion. Any necessary flow or congestion control must be implemented at the application level.

Error Checking and Recovery

UDP provides a checksum for error checking, but it doesn't have any mechanism for error recovery. If a datagram is found to have an error (indicated by the checksum), it's simply discarded. UDP doesn't provide acknowledgments of successful data receipt or retries for failed transmissions.

Despite its apparent lack of features, UDP is useful in situations where speed is more important than reliability or where the application itself provides reliability. Real-time applications like video streaming, VoIP, and online gaming often use UDP to reduce latency. DNS queries and network discovery protocols also use UDP due to its simplicity and the small size of data being transferred. While UDP may not offer the reliability and ordered delivery of TCP, its simplicity and speed make it a valuable tool in the network protocol toolkit. In the later part of this chapter, we will explore how to implement UDP communication in C++.

Comparing TCP and UDP – When to use Which?

TCP and UDP, as we've learned, are two core protocols used in network communication, but they offer very different services, each suited to particular types of applications and network scenarios.

Let us compare the two and understand when it is more appropriate to use one over the other.

Connection Orientation

TCP is a connection-oriented protocol, meaning a connection must be established between the sender and receiver before data transfer begins. This connection ensures that the network path and the required system resources are ready for communication.

In contrast, UDP is connectionless, allowing data packets, or datagrams, to be sent without establishing a connection. This makes UDP faster and more efficient for small, stateless exchanges.

Reliability

TCP is considered a reliable protocol because it ensures that all data sent arrives at the destination in the correct order. It achieves this by using sequence numbers and acknowledgments, retransmitting any packets that are lost or arrive out of order.

UDP, on the other hand, doesn't provide these mechanisms. It sends datagrams independently of each other, with no guarantee of delivery or correct sequencing. This lack of reliability is why UDP is often referred to as an "unreliable" protocol.

Flow Control and Congestion Control

TCP provides flow control, ensuring that a sender doesn't overwhelm a receiver by sending more data than it can handle. It also has congestion control to prevent network congestion by adjusting the data transmission rate based on network conditions.

UDP lacks both flow control and congestion control. It continually sends datagrams at the speed desired by the application, regardless of network conditions or the receiver's capacity.

Speed

Given its connection setup, reliability mechanisms, flow control, and congestion control, TCP is slower than UDP. It's best suited for applications where data integrity is more critical than speed.

UDP is faster due to its connectionless nature and lack of reliability, flow control, or congestion control. It's ideal for real-time applications where speed is crucial, and some data loss or out-of-order arrival is acceptable.

When to use TCP or UDP

The choice between TCP and UDP depends on the requirements of the application in question.

Use TCP when

- Data must be delivered in order and without errors.
- The network application can tolerate comparatively slower data delivery.
- The application does not need to manage the complexities of control mechanisms.
- Common uses include web browsing (HTTP/HTTPS), email (SMTP/POP/IMAP), and file transfers (FTP).

Use UDP when

- The application requires fast, efficient transmission, such as games or voice and video applications where lost packets are preferable to late packets.
- The application can handle packet sequencing and error checking.
- The data to be sent is small, such as DNS queries.

In an organizational context, network administrators must understand the nature of the network traffic and the needs of the application to choose between TCP and UDP. For instance, for real-time communication tools, UDP would be more suitable for maintaining speed, while for data backup services, TCP's reliability would be essential.

As we progress through this book, we will further explore programming network applications using both TCP and UDP with C++, offering a practical perspective on these considerations.

Sockets and Socket Programming

Before we dive into TCP and UDP programming in C++, we must first understand the concept of a socket. Sockets are a fundamental entity used in network programming for establishing communication between different processes over a network. They serve as an interface for programming networks at the transport layer of the internet protocol suite and can be created using various programming languages, including C++. Let us delve deeper into what sockets are and how they work in the realm of network programming.

What is a Socket?

A socket, in the context of networking, is an endpoint in a communication flow between two systems running network software. It can be seen as a communication gate. It has a socket number consisting of an IP address concatenated with a port number, e.g., '192.168.1.1:22' for an SSH server running on a machine with IP address 192.168.1.1. Port numbers allow different applications on the same machine to share a single IP address without interfering with each other's communication.

Socket Programming in C++

Socket programming is a method of communication between two computers using sockets. In C++, socket programming is done by using a series of system calls to make the network communication possible.

The process usually involves the following steps:

- Socket Creation: The socket function creates a new socket and returns a socket descriptor that can be used in later system calls. The socket is created using the socket(domain, type, protocol) function, where domain refers to the communication domain (usually AF_INET for IPv4 or AF_INET6 for IPv6), type refers to the communication type (SOCK_STREAM for TCP or SOCK_DGRAM for UDP), and protocol is usually set to 0 to automatically select the appropriate protocol based on the chosen type.

- Binding the Socket: Once the socket is created, it needs to be bound to a specific IP address and port number using the bind() function. This allows the socket to receive incoming data directed to that IP and port.

- Listening and Accepting Connections: In the case of server applications, the socket then listens for incoming connections using the listen() function, and when a client attempts to connect, the server accepts the connection using the accept() function.

- Connecting to a Server: For client applications, the socket attempts to connect to a server using the connect() function, specifying the server's IP address and port number.

- Data Transfer: Once a connection is established (either by accepting a client connection for a server or successfully connecting to a server for a client), data can be sent and received using the send() and recv() functions (or write() and read()).

- Closing the Socket: After the communication is finished, the socket must be closed using the close() function (or closesocket() on Windows).

C++ provides a rich library support for socket programming. In the coming chapters, we'll delve into practical aspects of socket programming with both TCP and UDP in C++ using the libraries as discussed in Chapter 1, providing hands-on examples and exercises for a better understanding. Understanding sockets and socket programming is fundamental for any network administrator, as it forms the basis of many network operations and applications.

TCP Client-Server Socket Programming

Let us put the theory we've learned in previous sections/chapter into practice by creating a simple TCP client-server application in C++. For this example, we'll be using the Boost.Asio library which provides a powerful, consistent, and expressive C++ interface for network programming.

Setting up Boost.Asio

Before we start, make sure you have the Boost.Asio library installed and configured in your development environment. Refer back to Chapter 1 if you need a refresher on how to do this.

Server Application

Below is a basic TCP echo server that receives data from a client, and sends the same data back to the client.

```
#include <boost/asio.hpp>
```

```
using boost::asio::ip::tcp;

int main() {
 try {
  boost::asio::io_service io_service;

  tcp::acceptor acceptor(io_service, tcp::endpoint(tcp::v4(), 12345));

  for (;;) {
   tcp::socket socket(io_service);
   acceptor.accept(socket);

   std::array<char, 128> buf;
   boost::system::error_code error;

   while (true) {
    size_t len = socket.read_some(boost::asio::buffer(buf), error);

    if (error == boost::asio::error::eof)
     break;
    else if (error)
     throw boost::system::system_error(error);

    boost::asio::write(socket, boost::asio::buffer(buf, len));
   }
  }
 }
 catch (std::exception& e) {
  std::cerr << e.what() << std::endl;
 }

 return 0;
```

```
}
```

The server listens for new connections on port 12345. When a client connects, the server enters a loop where it reads data from the client and writes the same data back to the client.

Client Application

Next, we create the corresponding TCP client that connects to the server, sends some data, and receives the response.

```
#include <boost/asio.hpp>
#include <iostream>

using boost::asio::ip::tcp;

int main() {
  try {
    boost::asio::io_service io_service;

    tcp::resolver resolver(io_service);
    tcp::resolver::query query(tcp::v4(), "localhost", "12345");
    tcp::resolver::iterator endpoint_iterator = resolver.resolve(query);

    tcp::socket socket(io_service);
    boost::asio::connect(socket, endpoint_iterator);

    const std::string msg = "Hello, World!\n";
    boost::asio::write(socket, boost::asio::buffer(msg, msg.size()));

    std::array<char, 128> buf;
    boost::system::error_code error;

    while (true) {
      size_t len = socket.read_some(boost::asio::buffer(buf), error);
```

```
    if (error == boost::asio::error::eof)
      break;
    else if (error)
      throw boost::system::system_error(error);

    std::cout.write(buf.data(), len);
  }
}
catch (std::exception& e) {
  std::cerr << e.what() << std::endl;
}

return 0;
}
```

The client connects to the server running on localhost on port 12345, sends a "Hello, World!\n" message, and then reads and prints the server's response.

The above program illustrates the basics of TCP client-server programming with sockets in C++ using the Boost.Asio library. In the next chapters, we will further enhance these programs to include more complex interactions and more advanced networking concepts.

UDP Client-Server Socket Programming

UDP, or User Datagram Protocol, is a connectionless protocol used for applications where speed and efficiency are important, and a little data loss is acceptable. Examples of UDP-based applications include DNS queries, video streaming, and online multiplayer gaming. Now, let us create a simple UDP echo server and client using the Boost.Asio library in C++.

Server Application

The server will receive datagrams from a client, and send the same data back to the client. Below is the basic code for the UDP echo server:

```
#include <boost/asio.hpp>
```

```
using boost::asio::ip::udp;

int main() {
  try {
    boost::asio::io_service io_service;

    udp::socket socket(io_service, udp::endpoint(udp::v4(), 12345));

    for (;;) {
      std::array<char, 1024> recv_buf;
      udp::endpoint remote_endpoint;
      boost::system::error_code error;
      size_t len = socket.receive_from(boost::asio::buffer(recv_buf),
remote_endpoint, 0, error);

      if (error && error != boost::asio::error::message_size)
        throw boost::system::system_error(error);

      boost::asio::send_to(socket, boost::asio::buffer(recv_buf, len),
remote_endpoint, 0, error);
    }
  }
  catch (std::exception& e) {
    std::cerr << e.what() << std::endl;
  }

  return 0;
}
```

The server is bound to port 12345, and it enters a loop where it waits to receive a datagram, and then sends the same datagram back to the client.

Client Application

Next, we create the corresponding UDP client that sends datagrams to the server and receives the response. Below is the basic code for the UDP client:

```
#include <boost/asio.hpp>
#include <iostream>

using boost::asio::ip::udp;

int main() {
  try {
    boost::asio::io_service io_service;

    udp::resolver resolver(io_service);
    udp::resolver::query query(udp::v4(), "localhost", "12345");
    udp::endpoint receiver_endpoint = *resolver.resolve(query);

    udp::socket socket(io_service);
    socket.open(udp::v4());

    std::array<char, 1024> send_buf = { "Hello, World!\n" };
    socket.send_to(boost::asio::buffer(send_buf, send_buf.size()),
receiver_endpoint);

    std::array<char, 1024> recv_buf;
    udp::endpoint sender_endpoint;

    size_t len = socket.receive_from(boost::asio::buffer(recv_buf),
sender_endpoint);

    std::cout.write(recv_buf.data(), len);
  }
  catch (std::exception& e) {
```

```
    std::cerr << e.what() << std::endl;
  }

  return 0;
}
```

The client sends a "Hello, World!\n" message to the server running on localhost on port 12345, and then reads and prints the server's response. Like the previous TCP examples, the error handling in these programs is kept minimal for clarity. By understanding both TCP and UDP client-server programming, you'll have a solid foundation to build upon for more advanced network programming tasks, and gain a practical understanding of the two primary transport protocols used in networked applications.

Socket Programming Best Practices

As with any programming discipline, there are best practices that can guide you in creating efficient, maintainable, and secure applications. Below are several important best practices for socket programming, particularly in the context of TCP and UDP:

- Error HandlingNetwork communication is inherently unreliable and subject to failures. Always handle errors that can occur during the different phases of network communication. For instance, check the return values of socket functions and handle exceptions where applicable. Provide useful and informative error messages to help with debugging and troubleshooting.

- Use Non-Blocking Sockets: Non-blocking sockets allow your application to continue doing other work while waiting for network operations to complete, improving performance and responsiveness. However, they also require more careful programming and error handling. Consider using asynchronous I/O libraries (like Boost.Asio in C++) which abstract away much of the complexity.

- Connection Handling: For TCP, ensure to handle connection termination properly. Both client and server should close the socket when they are done with the connection. Failure to properly close a connection can result in "resource leaks" which may eventually prevent new connections from being established.

- Buffer Management: Choose appropriate buffer sizes for sending and receiving data. If the buffer is too small, you will need to make more calls to send or receive data. If it's too large, you may waste memory. Often, a size of 1024 or 4096 bytes is a good starting point.

- Data Serialization and Parsing: When sending complex data structures over the network, you'll need to serialize the data to a format that can be sent over the network (such as JSON, XML, or binary), and then parse the data at the other end. Be careful to handle parsing errors, which can occur if the data is corrupted or not in the expected format.

- Handle Network Byte Order: Network protocols usually use big-endian byte order, which may be different from the byte order used by your computer's CPU (known as host byte order). Use functions like htons() (host to network short), htonl() (host to network long), ntohs() (network to host short), and ntohl() (network to host long) to convert between host and network byte order.

- Security Measures: Consider the security of your network applications. Use encryption for sensitive data, validate and sanitize input to protect against injection attacks, and consider using firewalls and other security measures to protect your server.

- Resource Management: Make sure to free any resources that your program allocates. This includes closing sockets after use, and freeing any dynamically allocated memory.

- Consider Scalability: If your server application needs to handle many connections, consider using a design that can scale well. This could involve using multi-threading or asynchronous I/O, depending on the needs of your application and the capabilities of your hardware.

- Testing: Make sure to thoroughly test your network applications. This includes testing with different types of network conditions, such as high latency or packet loss, to ensure your application can handle these situations gracefully.

By adhering to these best practices, you'll be well on your way to writing robust, efficient, and secure network applications with TCP and UDP in C++.

Summary

This Chapter opened with an in-depth exploration of Internet protocols, discussing their importance in contemporary networking and their role in efficient communication. The focus then shifted to TCP, where we unveiled its structure and explored its fundamental elements like handshake, connection, and termination. A thorough explanation of TCP enabled the reader to appreciate its reliability and its significance in the successful delivery of data over the network.

Following the detailed look at TCP, we moved onto UDP. Similar to TCP, we deconstructed its structure and functions, emphasizing its benefits and potential uses. This provided the reader with a nuanced understanding of how UDP works as a lightweight and speedy protocol that does not provide the same level of assurance as TCP but excels in applications where speed is prioritized. The chapter then led to a comparative study between TCP and UDP. The comparison aimed to highlight the differences and guide the readers to make informed decisions regarding the use of these protocols depending on their specific requirements. The contrast helped identify scenarios where one protocol would outperform the other, ensuring the efficient utilization of both protocols. The latter part of the chapter marked the introduction to sockets and socket programming in C++. It paved the way for an interactive session on TCP client-server socket programming, giving the reader a hands-on understanding of how to create a simple TCP server and client using the C++ libraries discussed in Chapter 1.

Finally, the chapter concluded with the best practices in socket programming for both TCP and UDP. These guidelines are designed to ensure the reader can create robust, efficient, and secure network applications. This chapter serves as a comprehensive guide to internet protocols and socket programming, laying a solid foundation for the forthcoming chapters on more complex networking tasks.

CHAPTER 3: NETWORK INTERFACES AND ADDRESSING

Overview of Network Interfaces and Addressing

A computer network is a group of interconnected devices that share data and resources. Within a network, devices communicate with each other using a system of digital signals. For a device to participate in a network, it needs a network interface and an address. A network interface is the point of interconnection between a computer and a private or public network. A network interface is usually a network interface card (NIC) with a software driver. The NIC provides a physical connection to the network. It often has an Ethernet port for wired connections and an antenna for wireless ones. The software driver enables the operating system and the network protocol to function together with the hardware.

All NICs have a unique identifier, called a Media Access Control (MAC) address. MAC addresses are assigned to the NIC at the time of manufacture and are stored in its hardware. An address in a network is a unique identifier assigned to each device on the network. It allows devices to send and receive information to and from specific devices.

There are two types of addressing schemes:

1) IP Addressing: An Internet Protocol (IP) address is a numerical label assigned to each device participating in a computer network that uses the Internet Protocol for communication. It serves two main functions: host or network interface identification and location addressing.

2) MAC Addressing: As mentioned, every network interface card has a unique MAC address that identifies it on the network at the physical layer of the network protocol.

There are two versions of IP addresses in use: IPv4 and IPv6. IPv4 addresses are 32 bits long, and IPv6 addresses are 128 bits long. The length of the IP address affects the total number of possible addresses. The IPv4 addressing system is organized into classes (A, B, C, D, E) for different kinds of networks, from small networks (fewer addresses, such as Class C) to large networks (more addresses, such as Class A). However, with the advent of CIDR (Classless Inter-Domain Routing), the concept of classes is no longer used. The topic of addressing is also linked to the concept of subnetting. Subnetting is a technique used to divide a network into two or more smaller network segments (called subnets), each functioning as a small, separate network. This improves network performance and provides security.

In the upcoming sections, we will dive deeper into subnetting, IP configuration, and programming network interfaces, which are essential for network administrators. These topics will help you understand how devices are assigned addresses, how network traffic is routed efficiently, and how you can interact with network interfaces programmatically using C++.

Understanding Network Interfaces

Network interfaces serve as the communication bridge between your computer and the network, enabling data transmission between your device and others on the network or internet. In this case, we'll delve into understanding network interfaces within the contexts of two prevalent operating systems: Windows and Linux.

Network Interfaces in Windows

Windows organizes network interfaces within the Network and Sharing Center, which provides a graphical interface to manage connections and view network information. You can access the Network and Sharing Center through the Control Panel.

Each network interface, be it a physical Ethernet port, a Wi-Fi adapter, or a virtual adapter (like those used in VPNs), is represented as a network connection. You can view and change properties, including IP addressing information, DNS server information, and more, by right-clicking a network connection and selecting "Properties".

Additionally, Windows has a powerful command-line tool for network troubleshooting and interface management called "netsh" (network shell). Using netsh, you can view interface settings, change IP addresses, and perform various other network-related tasks.

Network Interfaces in Linux

In Linux, network interfaces are traditionally managed using command-line tools. The specific tools can vary depending on the Linux distribution and version. The ifconfig command is traditionally used to display information about the network interfaces on the system, as well as to configure them. However, ifconfig is now deprecated in many Linux distributions. The ip command is now the preferred tool for network interface management on modern Linux systems. It can display information about network interfaces, and also configure them.

Network interfaces in Linux are typically named "eth0", "eth1", etc. for Ethernet connections, and "wlan0", "wlan1", etc. for wireless connections. Linux also supports a broad range of virtual network interfaces, such as loopback interfaces (lo), tunnel interfaces (tun/tap), and bridge interfaces (br).

IP Addresses and Subnets

IP Addresses

IP (Internet Protocol) addresses are unique identifiers assigned to each device in a network. In Linux, you generally interact with two versions of IP addresses: IPv4 and IPv6.

IPv4 is the most widely used version. An IPv4 address consists of four sets of numbers ranging from 0 to 255, separated by periods, for example, 192.168.1.1. These addresses are further divided into five classes (A, B, C, D, and E) based on the first octet's value.

IPv6 is the newer version, designed to address the limitation of available addresses in IPv4. An IPv6 address consists of eight sets of four hexadecimal digits, separated by colons, for example, 2001:0db8:85a3:0000:0000:8a2e:0370:7334.

Each network interface configured with an IP address has two components: the network address and the host address. The network address identifies the network, while the host address identifies a specific device on that network.

Subnets

Subnetting is a technique used to divide a network into smaller, more manageable pieces. Each of these pieces is known as a subnet. A subnet still behaves like a network; it has its own network address and range of host addresses.

Subnetting is essential for several reasons:

- It can reduce network congestion and increase network performance.
- It allows better control over network growth.
- It can isolate network issues, minimizing their impact.

The network part of the IP address, in conjunction with the subnet mask, defines the subnet. The subnet mask is a 32-bit number that masks an IP address and divides the IP address into network address and host address. The subnet mask is usually written as four octets, similar to an address. For example, a common subnet mask for a Class C IP address is 255.255.255.0, which means that 24 bits are used for the network. In CIDR notation, it's expressed as "/24" (pronounced "slash twenty-four"). When a device reads the IP address, it checks the subnet mask. Bits set to "1" in the mask represent the network, and those set to "0" represent the host.

The concept of IP addressing and subnetting is crucial in the world of networking. These concepts form the basis for data routing, network management, and network security. Understanding these concepts is vital for network administrators and programmers dealing with networking applications. In the following chapters, we'll explore how you can use C++ libraries to interact with and manipulate these components in Linux.

Perform Subnetting and IP Configuration

While C++ itself doesn't inherently provide tools for IP configuration or subnetting, it can interface with system tools that do, such as the 'ip' command in Linux. Also, using libraries like ASIO and POCO, we can create network applications that handle and manipulate IP addresses.

Below is an example of how you can use C++ and the ASIO library to retrieve and work with IP addresses:

Install Boost and ASIO

```
sudo apt-get install libboost-all-dev
```

Include necessary libraries in your C++ file:

```
#include <boost/asio.hpp>
#include <iostream>
```

Retrieve IP Address

To retrieve IP addresses of your network interfaces, you can use the ip::tcp::resolver class from ASIO:

```
boost::asio::io_service netService;
boost::asio::ip::tcp::resolver   resolver(netService);
boost::asio::ip::tcp::resolver::query query(boost::asio::ip::host_name(),"");
```

```
boost::asio::ip::tcp::resolver::iterator endpoints = resolver.resolve(query);
boost::asio::ip::tcp::resolver::iterator end;
for (; endpoints != end; ++endpoints) {
  std::cout << "IP: " << endpoints->endpoint().address() << "\n";
}
```

In this code, host_name() returns the host name of the system, and the resolver object queries network interfaces of the system.

Working with IP Addresses

Once you have retrieved IP addresses, you can work with them using the ip::address class in ASIO. For example, you can check whether an address is loopback, multicast, or IPv4/IPv6:

```
boost::asio::ip::address addr = endpoints->endpoint().address();
std::cout << "Is Loopback: " << addr.is_loopback() << "\n";
std::cout << "Is Multicast: " << addr.is_multicast() << "\n";
std::cout << "Is V4: " << addr.is_v4() << "\n";
std::cout << "Is V6: " << addr.is_v6() << "\n";
```

For actual subnetting or changing IP configuration, you would generally use system-specific commands (ip, ifconfig, etc.), which can be called from a C++ program using system() function. It is also worth mentioning that ASIO and other similar libraries can work with IP addresses and ports to create network applications, which is where they are usually used. They provide functionalities to create servers and clients, send and receive data, handle multiple connections simultaneously, etc.

In the next sections, we'll look into creating a simple server and client, which will give you a practical sense of how networking works in C++.

Create TCP Server and Client

Let us start with creating a simple TCP server and client using Boost.Asio library, as it is one of the most popular C++ libraries for network programming.

Creating a Simple TCP Server

The server waits for a client to connect, reads data sent by the client, and then sends a response back.

Below is a basic TCP server that echoes whatever it receives from a client:

```
#include <boost/asio.hpp>

using boost::asio::ip::tcp;

int main()
{
   boost::asio::io_service io_service;

   tcp::acceptor acceptor(io_service, tcp::endpoint(tcp::v4(), 1234));

   for (;;)
   {
      tcp::socket socket(io_service);
      acceptor.accept(socket);

      std::string data = "Hello from server!";
      boost::system::error_code ignored_error;
      boost::asio::write(socket, boost::asio::buffer(data), ignored_error);
   }
}
```

In this code:

- A tcp::acceptor object is created to accept new connections.
- It waits indefinitely for clients to connect with the acceptor.accept(socket); line. Once a client connects, it sends a message back to the client.

Creating a Simple TCP Client

The client connects to the server, sends some data, and reads the server's response.

Below is a simple TCP client that sends a message to the server and prints the server's response:

```
#include <boost/asio.hpp>
#include <iostream>

using boost::asio::ip::tcp;

int main()
{
    boost::asio::io_service io_service;

    tcp::resolver resolver(io_service);
    tcp::resolver::query query("localhost", "1234");
    tcp::resolver::iterator endpoint_iterator = resolver.resolve(query);

    tcp::socket socket(io_service);
    boost::asio::connect(socket, endpoint_iterator);

    std::string message = "Hello from client!";
    boost::system::error_code ignored_error;
    boost::asio::write(socket, boost::asio::buffer(message), ignored_error);

    char reply[1024];
    size_t reply_length = boost::asio::read(socket, boost::asio::buffer(reply,1024),
ignored_error);
    std::cout << "Reply is: ";
    std::cout.write(reply, reply_length);
    std::cout << "\n";
```

```
    return 0;
}
```

In this code:

- tcp::resolver::query is used to specify the server's address and port number.
- tcp::socket is used to create a socket and boost::asio::connect to connect it to the server.
- It then sends a message to the server and waits for a response.
- The server's response is read into a buffer and then printed out.

Please remember to run the server before the client. You can compile and run these C++ files separately. This example gives you a starting point to understand how networking works in C++.

Common Challenges in TCP/UDP Connections

Creating a robust client-server application requires understanding and handling several common network errors. Errors can arise from various sources, such as network issues, software bugs, system resource limits, or incorrect usage by clients.

Below are some of the most common errors you might encounter when establishing TCP and UDP connections and their general solutions.

1. Connection Refused: This error typically occurs when trying to connect to a port where no service is listening. This could mean that the server is not running, or the server process is not configured to listen on the specified port. Make sure the server is running and listening on the correct port.

2. Connection Timeout: If the server is unresponsive or the network is slow or congested, the client's connection request may timeout. In this case, you can increase the connection timeout value. If the problem persists, you need to diagnose the network or server performance issues.

3. Address Already in Use: This error means another socket on the same host is

already bound to the specified port. This could happen if a previous instance of your server has not released the port yet. It's common when a server crashes and then quickly restarts. Enable the SO_REUSEADDR socket option to allow immediate reuse of the port.

4. Network Unreachable: If the client's network isn't able to reach the server's network, you'll get a "network unreachable" error. This usually indicates a routing problem or a network outage. Check the network connectivity and routing.

5. Insufficient Resources: If the system or process runs out of resources like file descriptors, memory, or CPU, you may see errors like "Too many open files" or "Cannot allocate memory". In these cases, you need to manage system resources more efficiently or increase system limits.

6. Software Caused Connection Abort: This error happens when a connection is lost while data is being sent or received. It can be due to network issues, or the client or server unexpectedly closing the connection. Implement appropriate error-handling and retry logic in your code.

When using Boost.Asio or other similar libraries in C++, network errors are usually reported through boost::system::error_code objects. You can use the message() member function of error_code to get a human-readable string explaining the error:

```
boost::system::error_code ec;
// Some operation that sets ec...
if (ec) {
   std::cerr << "Error: " << ec.message() << "\n";
}
```

Remember that it's important to handle errors properly in your code, especially in network applications. Unhandled errors can lead to resource leaks, application crashes, and security vulnerabilities.

Summary

To sum up the learnings, we dug deeper into the network interfaces and addressed the conceptual understanding of IP addresses and Subnets. A comprehensive overview of network interfaces on Windows and Linux platforms was provided, helping you grasp the functionalities and roles these interfaces play in a networking context. We also introduced the vital concepts around IP addresses and subnetting, setting the stage for a better understanding of network infrastructure.

We then moved onto the practical aspects of performing subnetting and IP configuration. While C++ doesn't inherently provide tools for IP configuration or subnetting, we demonstrated how it could interface with system tools and libraries like ASIO and POCO. This covered everything from retrieving and working with IP addresses to invoking system-specific commands for modifying network settings. A note of caution was also given about the potential security implications of changing network settings directly from a C++ program.

Finally, we explored creating a simple server-client setup and standard device interactions using C++. Detailed, step-by-step guidance was provided for setting up a TCP server and client using Boost.Asio. The chapter concluded with a discussion on common errors that occur in establishing TCP and UDP client-server connections and how to handle them effectively. All in all, the chapter has equipped you with fundamental skills to start exploring more advanced networking tasks in C++.

CHAPTER 4: APPLICATION LAYER PROTOCOLS

Application Layer

The Application Layer is the highest level in the Open System Interconnection (OSI) model and the Internet Protocol Suite (TCP/IP model), which are the conceptual models that describe how different network protocols interact and work together to provide network services. It is where network applications and user processes live, and it's where human-network interaction occurs. The primary purpose of the Application Layer is to provide a set of interfaces for applications to obtain access to network services, which could be as simple as transferring files or as complex as electronic commerce. It provides protocols and services to facilitate communication among applications, abstracting the complexities of the network stack below it.

Protocols in the Application Layer are closest to the end-user and enable the user to interact with the network. These protocols are designed to provide user-friendly interfaces and to provide a variety of services to the user, such as email (SMTP, IMAP), file transfer (FTP), web browsing (HTTP, HTTPS), and domain name resolution (DNS), among others. An important characteristic of the Application Layer is that it is host to network-agnostic protocols. These protocols can operate on top of any transport layer protocol, such as Transmission Control Protocol (TCP) or User Datagram Protocol (UDP).

As a network administrator or a network-oriented developer, understanding the Application Layer protocols is crucial because they directly impact the functionality and performance of network services. Proper comprehension aids in troubleshooting network problems, optimizing network performance, and developing new network applications or services.

Now that we've introduced the Application Layer, we can delve into the specific protocols like HTTP, HTTPS, FTP, SMTP, IMAP, and DNS

HTTP (HyperText Transfer Protocol)

The Hypertext Transfer Protocol (HTTP) is a fundamental and stateless protocol primarily utilized in the World Wide Web to facilitate communication between client systems and servers. This client-server protocol operates by processing requests sent by clients to servers, followed by appropriate responses from the servers. This request-response model is instrumental in exchanging HTML documents and a multitude of other web-based resources.

HTTP, under the hood, leverages the Transmission Control Protocol (TCP) as its backbone transport protocol. This combination assures reliable and ordered delivery of data packets over the network. The HTTP protocol comprises various methods such as

GET, POST, DELETE, and PUT, each serving a unique purpose in the request and retrieval of diverse types of web resources. However, a significant shortcoming of HTTP is its lack of encryption. The absence of encryption implies that data, including potentially sensitive information, is transmitted over the network in plain text, which exposes it to eavesdropping and data theft. Therefore, HTTP often necessitates additional security mechanisms to safeguard data during transmission.

HTTPS (HyperText Transfer Protocol Secure)

HTTPS, standing for Hypertext Transfer Protocol Secure, is essentially an enhanced and secure version of HTTP, which is used for data communication over the internet. Its primary purpose is to provide a secure environment for information exchange by encrypting the data transmitted between a client, typically a web browser, and a server. This encryption is achieved through a protocol known as Transport Layer Security (TLS), and previously, its predecessor, Secure Sockets Layer (SSL).

By using HTTPS, the information exchanged becomes nearly impossible to be intercepted or manipulated by third parties, thereby ensuring data integrity and confidentiality. This encryption is particularly crucial when handling sensitive information like credit card details, social security numbers, and login credentials, making HTTPS a standard requirement for websites dealing with such data. Moreover, the usage of HTTPS has extended beyond just sensitive sites, becoming a best practice for all websites to build trust with their users and to improve their search engine rankings.

FTP (File Transfer Protocol)

File Transfer Protocol, or FTP, is a tried-and-true method for moving files between systems across the internet. It's a standard network protocol that functions based on the client-server model. In this model, the client initiates a connection to a server, after which file transfer can commence. One defining feature of FTP is its use of two separate connections for control and data. The control connection is used for sending commands and receiving responses, while the actual data is transferred through the data connection.

A distinctive characteristic of FTP is its clear-text authentication system, which usually requires a username and password. However, this can pose a security risk as the login details are sent in an unencrypted form, making it vulnerable to network sniffing. FTP is used extensively worldwide, despite the advent of more secure alternatives, because of its simplicity and widespread support. Despite its vulnerabilities, FTP continues to be a critical part of the internet's infrastructure.

SMTP (Simple Mail Transfer Protocol)

Simple Mail Transfer Protocol, commonly known as SMTP, is a well-established standard protocol dedicated to the transmission of e-mail messages across servers in a network. It functions primarily over the Internet, serving as the backbone of any email delivery system by facilitating the transfer of emails between server systems. Regardless of the size or complexity of the mail system, the majority, if not all, utilize SMTP to handle outbound mail transport.

The protocol serves a dual purpose: it's also employed to send messages from an email client, such as Outlook or Thunderbird, to a mail server for further routing. Once the messages are successfully transmitted and stored on the recipient's mail server, they can be fetched and read using an email client. This retrieval is typically carried out using either the Post Office Protocol (POP) or the Internet Message Access Protocol (IMAP), which are responsible for accessing and managing the messages stored on the server. Thus, SMTP plays a crucial role in the overall email communication process.

IMAP (Internet Message Access Protocol)

Internet Message Access Protocol (IMAP) is an essential internet standard protocol that plays a pivotal role in managing and retrieving emails from a mail server. Unlike its predecessor, POP3, which necessitates downloading emails to a local system, IMAP allows users to access their email messages directly on the server. This distinctive feature offers users the convenience of accessing their emails from any device, provided they have internet connectivity. Moreover, IMAP enables simultaneous access from multiple clients or client "sessions", fostering robust multi-device accessibility. Users can interact with their mailstore from various devices concurrently without any conflict, offering immense flexibility and productivity in an interconnected world.

The IMAP protocol is primarily designed to provide real-time, synchronised access to emails, making it a crucial tool for individuals and businesses alike. Whether you're checking messages from your desktop at work, smartphone on the go, or tablet at home, IMAP ensures your emails are consistently available, and changes made are universally reflected. This simultaneous, real-time access capability distinguishes IMAP as an indispensable component of modern email systems.

DNS (Domain Name System)

DNS is a hierarchical decentralized naming system for computers, services, or other resources connected to the Internet or a private network. It translates human-readable domain names (like www.google.com) into the numerical IP addresses needed for locating and identifying computer services and devices. This is essential because while computers and network hardware work with IP addresses to determine where information should be sent, people find it much easier to work with names than numeric addresses.

Each of these protocols is essential to various aspects of internet communication and has its own specific purpose and set of rules for communication. Understanding them is critical for network programming, especially when it comes to interacting with web servers, mail servers, file servers, and DNS servers.

HTTP and HTTPS Deep Dive

HTTP (HyperText Transfer Protocol) is an application-layer protocol used primarily for transmitting documents on the World Wide Web. HTTP follows a client-server model where the client opens a connection and sends a message to a known server. The server then responds with a message of its own and closes the connection.

HTTP messages consist of requests from client to server and responses from server to client. A request consists of a method (like GET or POST), the URL being requested, and a series of headers. A response consists of a response code (like 200 for success, 404 for not found), a message, and the response's own series of headers.

HTTPS (HTTP Secure) is the secure version of HTTP. It uses TLS (Transport Layer Security), or formerly SSL (Secure Sockets Layer), to encrypt the connection between the client and the server. This means all data sent between the two are fully encrypted, making it difficult for hackers to intercept and understand the data.

Send HTTP Request using Boost Beast

Now, let us dive into making HTTP/HTTPS requests using C++ with the help of the Boost Beast library which is part of Boost.Asio.

Below is a simple program that sends an HTTP GET request to an HTTP server:

```
#include <boost/beast/core.hpp>
#include <boost/beast/http.hpp>
#include <boost/asio/connect.hpp>
#include <boost/asio/ip/tcp.hpp>
#include <iostream>
#include <string>
```

```
namespace http = boost::beast::http;
namespace net = boost::asio;
using tcp = net::ip::tcp;

int main()
{
    try
    {
        auto const host = "example.com";
        auto const port = "80";
        auto const target = "/index.html";
        int version = 11;

        net::io_context ioc;

        tcp::resolver resolver(ioc);
        auto const results = resolver.resolve(host, port);

        tcp::socket socket(ioc);
        net::connect(socket, results.begin(), results.end());

        http::request<http::string_body> req{ http::verb::get, target, version };
        req.set(http::field::host, host);
        req.set(http::field::user_agent, BOOST_BEAST_VERSION_STRING);

        http::write(socket, req);

        boost::beast::flat_buffer buffer;
        http::response<http::dynamic_body> res;
        http::read(socket, buffer, res);

        std::cout << res << std::endl;
```

```
    socket.shutdown(tcp::socket::shutdown_both);
  }
  catch (std::exception const& e)
  {
    std::cerr << "Error: " << e.what() << std::endl;
    return EXIT_FAILURE;
  }

  return EXIT_SUCCESS;
}
```

This program sets up a connection to example.com on port 80 (the standard port for HTTP), sends a GET request for /index.html, and then reads and prints out the response.

For HTTPS support, you need to use the Boost Asio SSL module to create an SSL socket, which is somewhat more involved.

Using Boost Asio SSL for HTTPS request

Making an HTTPS request is a bit more complex than HTTP due to the SSL/TLS handshake that needs to happen for the secure connection. However, Boost Asio provides a convenient ssl::stream class which works as a wrapper around an existing stream (like a TCP socket) and adds SSL/TLS functionality to it.

Before we get into the code, please note that the Boost Asio SSL module relies on the OpenSSL library. You'll need to install OpenSSL and link against it in your project. Also ensure that your system has a certificate store available that OpenSSL can use to verify certificates.

Below is a simplified example of making an HTTPS GET request using Boost Asio and Boost Beast:

```
#include <boost/asio.hpp>
#include <boost/asio/ssl.hpp>
#include <boost/beast/http.hpp>
#include <iostream>
```

```
namespace http = boost::beast::http;
namespace net = boost::asio;
namespace ssl = net::ssl;
using tcp = net::ip::tcp;

int main()
{
    try
    {
        auto const host = "example.com";
        auto const port = "443";
        auto const target = "/index.html";
        int version = 11;

        net::io_context ioc;

        ssl::context ctx{ssl::context::tlsv12_client};

        // This holds the root certificate used for verification
        ctx.set_default_verify_paths();

        tcp::resolver resolver{ioc};
        auto const results = resolver.resolve(host, port);

        ssl::stream<tcp::socket> stream{ioc, ctx};
        net::connect(stream.next_layer(), results.begin(), results.end());

        stream.handshake(ssl::stream_base::client);

        http::request<http::string_body> req{http::verb::get, target, version};
        req.set(http::field::host, host);
        req.set(http::field::user_agent, BOOST_BEAST_VERSION_STRING);
```

```
    http::write(stream, req);

    boost::beast::flat_buffer buffer;
    http::response<http::dynamic_body> res;
    http::read(stream, res);

    std::cout << res << std::endl;

    stream.shutdown();
  }
  catch(std::exception const& e)
  {
    std::cerr << "Error: " << e.what() << std::endl;
    return EXIT_FAILURE;
  }

  return EXIT_SUCCESS;
}
```

This program works similarly to the HTTP example, but there are a few key differences:

We use ssl::stream<tcp::socket> instead of tcp::socket. This provides SSL/TLS functionality on top of the TCP socket.

We call stream.handshake(ssl::stream_base::client) to perform the SSL/TLS handshake before we send the HTTP request.

We call stream.shutdown() to cleanly close the SSL/TLS connection after we're done. One thing I would like to tell you is that this program will not verify the server's certificate by default. For proper certificate verification, you would have to call ctx.set_verify_mode(ssl::verify_peer), and use a ssl::rfc2818_verification object to verify the server's identity.

FTP Deep Dive

FTP (File Transfer Protocol) is a standard network protocol used for the transfer of computer files between a client and server on a computer network. FTP is built on a client-server model architecture using separate control and data connections between the client and the server.

FTP users may authenticate themselves with a clear-text sign-in protocol, normally in the form of a username and password, but can connect anonymously if the server is configured to allow it. FTP commands can be used to change directories, change the transfer mode between binary and text, download, upload, rename, delete files, etc.

Implement FTP using Curl

Below is an example of how you might implement basic FTP functionality in C++ using the C++ Curl library:

```
#include <iostream>
#include <curl/curl.h>

int main()
{
  CURL *curl;
  CURLcode res;
  std::string ftpUrl = "ftp://example.com/myfile.txt";
  std::string username = "myusername";
  std::string password = "mypassword";
  std::string ftpCommand = "RNFR myfile.txt";
  std::string renameCommand = "RNTO newfile.txt";

  curl_global_init(CURL_GLOBAL_DEFAULT);

  curl = curl_easy_init();
  if(curl) {
    struct curl_slist *headerlist=NULL;
    headerlist = curl_slist_append(headerlist, ftpCommand.c_str());
```

```
        headerlist = curl_slist_append(headerlist, renameCommand.c_str());

        curl_easy_setopt(curl, CURLOPT_URL, ftpUrl.c_str());

        curl_easy_setopt(curl, CURLOPT_USERNAME, username.c_str());
        curl_easy_setopt(curl, CURLOPT_PASSWORD, password.c_str());

        curl_easy_setopt(curl, CURLOPT_POSTQUOTE, headerlist);

        res = curl_easy_perform(curl);

        if(res != CURLE_OK)
            fprintf(stderr, "curl_easy_perform() failed: %s\n",
                    curl_easy_strerror(res));

        curl_slist_free_all (headerlist);

        curl_easy_cleanup(curl);
    }

    curl_global_cleanup();
    return 0;
}
```

This demonstrates how to use C++ and libcurl to rename a file (myfile.txt to newfile.txt) on an FTP server. In this code, we're using the CURLOPT_POSTQUOTE option to pass the FTP commands to libcurl. The command RNFR is used to specify the old name of the file, and RNTO is used to specify the new name.

Before you can use this code, you'll need to have libcurl installed and replace ftp://example.com/myfile.txt, myusername, and mypassword with the actual FTP server URL, username, and password.

SMTP & IMAP Deep Dive

SMTP (Simple Mail Transfer Protocol) is a communication protocol for electronic mail transmission. It's a mechanism used by mail servers to send and receive email messages. When you send an email, it's transferred over the Internet from one server to another using SMTP.

IMAP (Internet Message Access Protocol) on the other hand is a protocol used by email clients to retrieve messages from a mail server. When you check your inbox, your email client contacts the server using IMAP to fetch your emails.

In C++, you can use the VMime library for sending (SMTP) and receiving (IMAP) emails. VMime is a powerful C++ class library for parsing, generating, or editing Internet RFC-[2]822 and MIME messages. VMime is designed to provide a fast and an easy way to manipulate Internet mail messages.

Send Email using Vmime Library

Below is a simple example of how to send an email with VMime:

```
#include <vmime/vmime.hpp>
#include <vmime/platforms/posix/posixHandler.hpp>

int main() {
   vmime::platform::setHandler<vmime::platforms::posix::posixHandler>();

   // Constructs a new message
   vmime::shared_ptr<vmime::message> msg =
vmime::make_shared<vmime::message>();

   // Fill in the basic fields
   msg->getHeader()->getSubject()->setValue("Test mail");
   msg->getHeader()->getFrom()-
>appendAddress(vmime::make_shared<vmime::mailbox>("me@example.com"));
   msg->getHeader()->getTo()-
>appendAddress(vmime::make_shared<vmime::mailbox>("you@example.com"));
```

```
    // Message body
    vmime::shared_ptr<vmime::textContent> txt =
vmime::make_shared<vmime::textContent>("Hello, world!");

    msg->getBody()->setContents(txt);

    // Now, let's create the SMTP transport service
    vmime::shared_ptr<vmime::net::session> sess = vmime::net::session::create();

    vmime::shared_ptr<vmime::net::transport> tr = sess->getTransport("smtp",
"smtp.example.com");

    // Connect to server
    tr->connect();

    // Send the message
    tr->send(msg);

    // Disconnect
    tr->disconnect();

    return 0;
}
```

This program teaches you to send an email using VMime.

Receive Emails using VMime

And now, let us see a simple example of how to receive emails with VMime:

```
#include <vmime/vmime.hpp>
#include <vmime/platforms/posix/posixHandler.hpp>

int main() {
```

```
    vmime::platform::setHandler<vmime::platforms::posix::posixHandler>();

    // Now, let's create the IMAP store service
    vmime::shared_ptr<vmime::net::session> sess = vmime::net::session::create();

    vmime::shared_ptr<vmime::net::store> st = sess->getStore("imap",
"imap.example.com");

    // Connect to server
    st->connect();

    // Open the inbox folder
    vmime::shared_ptr<vmime::net::folder> f = st->getDefaultFolder()-
>getFolder("inbox");

    f->open(vmime::net::folder::MODE_READ_WRITE);

    // Get the message count
    int count = f->getMessageCount();

    std::cout << "You have " << count << " message(s)." << std::endl;

    // Disconnect
    st->disconnect();

    return 0;
}
```

This program teaches you to check the number of messages in an IMAP mailbox using VMime.

Before you can use the code examples, you'll need to have VMime linked in your project and replace smtp.example.com and imap.example.com with the actual SMTP and IMAP server URLs, and me@example.com and you@example.com with the actual email addresses.

Both SMTP and IMAP may require authentication, so you may need to use the setProperty() method to set your username and password. For example:

```
tr->setProperty("options.need-authentication", true);
tr->setProperty("auth.username", "myusername");
tr->setProperty("auth.password", "mypassword");
```

```
st->setProperty("options.need-authentication", true);
st->setProperty("auth.username", "myusername");
st->setProperty("auth.password", "mypassword");
```

Please note, these are plain text passwords. In a production environment, you should take care to secure them appropriately.

Also, keep in mind that not all mail servers are configured the same way, and may require specific settings or features. For example, Gmail requires you to enable "Less Secure Apps" to use basic SMTP/IMAP without OAuth2.

To wrap up, we've explored the basic structure of SMTP and IMAP protocols and demonstrated how to practically send and receive emails using the VMime library in C++. As these examples show, the VMime library provides a powerful and flexible interface for dealing with emails in C++.

DNS Deep Dive

The Domain Name System (DNS) operates as the internet's equivalent of a phone book. It's a service designed to translate easily understood domain names, such as "www.google.com," into numerical IP addresses which computers use to locate each other on the network. This translation process facilitates human-computer interaction, making it easier for users to navigate the web without having to remember complex numerical addresses.

DNS primarily operates using both TCP and UDP port 53, which provides flexibility and reliability to handle various types of requests. The system comprises four key components. DNS clients, also known as "resolvers," initiate the DNS lookup process. DNS servers then process these lookups, translating the domain names into IP addresses. DNS zones are administrative spaces for managing the domains under a single or multiple DNS servers.

Lastly, DNS records, stored in zones, hold key information about the domain, such as IP addresses (A records), mail servers (MX records), or aliases (CNAME records). This system ensures seamless internet navigation.

Types of DNS Queries

There are several types of DNS queries:

- Recursive query: In a recursive query, the DNS client demands a complete answer to the query, and the DNS server must return the IP address or an error message.
- Iterative query: In an iterative query, the DNS server returns the best answer it can using its local DNS database. If it doesn't have a match, it returns a referral to a DNS server authoritative for a lower level of the domain namespace.
- Non-recursive query: Non-recursive queries are usually sent by DNS servers to other DNS servers, rather than by clients.

The Boost ASIO library in C++ provides functionality for performing asynchronous DNS queries.

Perform DNS Query using Boost ASIO

Below is a simplified demonstration of how to perform a DNS query using Boost ASIO:

```
#include <boost/asio.hpp>
#include <iostream>

int main() {
  try {
      boost::asio::io_context io_context;

      boost::asio::ip::tcp::resolver resolver(io_context);
      boost::asio::ip::tcp::resolver::query query("www.google.com", "");

      boost::asio::ip::tcp::resolver::iterator endpoint_iterator =
resolver.resolve(query);
```

```
    for ( ; endpoint_iterator != boost::asio::ip::tcp::resolver::iterator();
++endpoint_iterator) {
        boost::asio::ip::tcp::endpoint endpoint = *endpoint_iterator;
        std::cout << endpoint << std::endl;
    }
  }
  catch (std::exception& e) {
    std::cerr << "Exception: " << e.what() << "\n";
  }

  return 0;
}
```

This code will print out the IP addresses associated with "www.google.com". The program creates a resolver object, uses it to resolve a query, and then prints out the resulting endpoints.

Error Handling in Socket Programming

Error handling is a crucial aspect of any programming task, and socket programming is no exception. C++ exceptions provide a powerful and flexible tool for propagating error conditions out of functions. When dealing with network programming in C++, especially when using libraries like Boost.Asio, it's important to be aware of and handle the exceptions and errors that may arise.

Common socket errors include:

- ECONNREFUSED: The target machine refused the connection request. This can occur if there's no server listening at the target address.

- ETIMEDOUT: The connection request timed out. This can occur if the server is too busy to accept new connections.

- EHOSTUNREACH and ENETUNREACH: The target host or network is unreachable. This can occur due to various network issues.
- EADDRINUSE: The local address is already in use. This occurs when you try to bind a socket to an IP address/port that's already in use.

- ECONNRESET and EPIPE: The connection was forcibly closed by the peer. This occurs when the server closes the connection, typically due to a timeout.

In C++, you can catch and handle these errors like this:

```
try {
  // Socket operations...
}
catch (boost::system::system_error& e) {
  if (e.code() == boost::asio::error::connection_refused) {
    std::cerr << "Connection refused" << std::endl;
  } else if (e.code() == boost::asio::error::timed_out) {
    std::cerr << "Connection timed out" << std::endl;
  } else if (e.code() == boost::asio::error::host_unreachable) {
    std::cerr << "Host unreachable" << std::endl;
  } else if (e.code() == boost::asio::error::address_in_use) {
    std::cerr << "Address in use" << std::endl;
  } else if (e.code() == boost::asio::error::connection_reset ||
        e.code() == boost::asio::error::broken_pipe) {
    std::cerr << "Connection forcibly closed by peer" << std::endl;
  } else {
    std::cerr << "Other error: " << e.what() << std::endl;
  }
}
```

In addition to handling system errors, you should also pay attention to application-level errors such as invalid protocol, incorrect message format, etc., and handle them appropriately based on the application logic.

Summary

In this chapter, we delved into the world of Application Layer Protocols and their practical use through C++. We began with an understanding of the Application Layer itself, appreciating its role as a bridge between network services and the applications that use them. We learned that protocols such as HTTP/HTTPS, FTP, SMTP, IMAP, and DNS function at this layer, providing the basis for the internet's most common tasks, from browsing the web to sending emails.

Next, we took a detailed look at each of these protocols, beginning with HTTP/HTTPS. We saw how they are utilized for accessing and sending data over the internet, using Boost.Asio and Boost.Asio SSL for HTTPS requests. FTP's role in file transfers was explored next, learning how to execute FTP operations using respective C++ libraries. We followed this with a study of SMTP and IMAP, the protocols essential for email transmission and retrieval. Practical demonstrations of sending and receiving emails using the VMime library in C++ were provided. Lastly, we unraveled DNS, which translates domain names to IP addresses, and learned to perform DNS queries using Boost Asio.

Lastly, we underscored the importance of error handling in socket programming, discussing common errors that might occur when dealing with TCP and UDP sockets, such as connection refusal and timeout errors. We detailed how these errors can be caught and handled in C++, ensuring the stability and security of our networking applications. This chapter's knowledge lays a strong foundation for any aspiring network administrator to understand the nuances of networking protocols and apply them in C++, making them a vital asset to any organization.

CHAPTER 5: VPNs

Introduction to Virtual Private Networks

Overview

Virtual Private Networks, or VPNs, are essential tools in the world of digital communication and data exchange. A VPN allows for a secure connection between a device and a network over the internet, encrypting data that is transferred across this connection to protect it from prying eyes. This is especially important in our increasingly interconnected world, where threats to data security and privacy are ever-present.

In the early days of the internet, network traffic was relatively easy to intercept. The need for secure communication led to the development of VPNs as a solution to this problem. VPNs were first introduced in the late 1990s and have grown in popularity ever since. They have become a staple in the corporate world, allowing remote workers to connect securely to their company's network. The rise of cybercrime, coupled with an increasing awareness of the importance of privacy, has further spurred the growth of VPN use among individual internet users.

VPNs are essential because they help ensure that the data exchanged between two points is private and inaccessible to others on the same network. This is incredibly important in a world where public Wi-Fi networks are ubiquitous, and threats such as man-in-the-middle attacks are prevalent. Furthermore, VPNs provide a way to bypass geographical restrictions on content. By rerouting the internet connection through a server in a different country, users can access content that would otherwise be blocked in their location. This has become increasingly important with the rise of streaming services that restrict content by region.

Components of VPN

A Virtual Private Network (VPN) is composed of multiple fundamental components that work together to establish secure, private connections over the internet.

A typical VPN consists of several components:

- VPN Client: This is the software installed on the user's device, which is used to establish and manage the VPN connection. The client encrypts and decrypts the data as it is sent and received.

- VPN Server: The VPN server is the endpoint of the VPN tunnel. It is responsible for encrypting and decrypting data sent by the VPN client.

- VPN Tunnel: This is the secure path through which the data travels. The tunnel protects the data from being seen or accessed while in transit.

- Internet Service Provider (ISP): While not a part of the VPN itself, the ISP is an essential player in the process. All data, encrypted or not, must be sent through the ISP. The difference is that, with a VPN, the ISP can see that data is being sent and received, but not the content of the data.

- Security Protocols: These are the cryptographic protocols that protect the data. Common examples include IPsec, L2TP, PPTP, and OpenVPN. They are responsible for creating the secure connection and ensuring that the data remains private.

In the chapters to follow, we will delve deeper into the world of VPNs, learning more about their functionality, their uses, and how to set them up and manage them with the aid of C++.

Applications of VPN

VPNs are a fundamental tool in today's business environment, used in a myriad of ways to improve security, accessibility, and privacy.

1) Secure Remote Access: The primary function of a VPN is to provide secure remote access to an organization's network. Given the rise of remote work, particularly in the wake of global events like the COVID-19 pandemic, VPNs have become essential for maintaining business continuity. Employees can access files, applications, and services as if they were physically present in the office, without compromising on security.

2) Data Protection: Cybersecurity is a significant concern in today's digital landscape. VPNs add a vital layer of security by encrypting data in transit, making it unreadable to any potential interceptors. This is particularly crucial when employees use public Wi-Fi networks, which are generally insecure and susceptible to attacks.

3) Inter-Office Communication: Organizations with multiple offices often use site-to-site VPNs to securely connect their networks. This enables seamless collaboration and resource sharing across different locations. It's akin to having a single, secure, private network that spans the entire organization.

4) Regulatory Compliance: Certain industries (like healthcare and finance) face strict regulations regarding data handling and privacy. A VPN can help businesses stay compliant by providing secure, encrypted communication.

5) Geolocation and IP Masking: By routing traffic through a server in a different location, a VPN can mask the user's IP address and make it appear as if they are browsing from a different geographical location. This can be used to access geographically restricted content or to conduct market research and testing in specific regions without physically being there.

6) Network Scalability: As businesses grow, so does the need for secure network infrastructure. Traditional private networks can be costly to scale. VPNs, on the other hand, leverage the infrastructure of the public internet, making them a more cost-effective solution for expanding businesses.

7) Vendor Access: Sometimes, third-party vendors need access to a company's network for maintenance, software updates, or other tasks. VPNs can provide temporary network access to vendors while keeping the rest of the network secure.

VPNs are thus a multifaceted tool in modern businesses, addressing several concerns around security, remote access, and regulatory compliance. The flexibility and security offered by VPNs make them a mainstay in today's digital world, one that's only set to grow as remote and flexible work arrangements become more common.

Types of VPN

A Virtual Private Network (VPN) can be deployed in two main ways: as a Remote Access VPN or a Site-to-Site VPN. Each serves a different purpose and is used in different scenarios.

Site-to-Site VPN

A Site-to-Site VPN, also known as a Router-to-Router VPN, is used when different offices of the same company need to connect to each other over the internet securely. In this setup, each location has a VPN gateway, like a router, firewall, or VPN concentrator, which is responsible for encrypting and decrypting the data coming in and out of the network.

There are two types of Site-to-Site VPNs:

1. Intranet-based Site-to-Site VPN: When a company has several remote locations that they want to join in a single private network, they create an intranet VPN. In this case, the network in each location is connected to the VPN gateway. This setup allows all offices to share resources as if they were on the same local network.

2. Extranet-based Site-to-Site VPN: Suppose a company wants to communicate and collaborate securely with an external company, like a supplier or a partner. In that

case, they can set up an extranet VPN. The external company won't have access to all the resources on the network, only the ones that are necessary for collaboration.

Remote Access VPN

A Remote Access VPN, also known as a Virtual Private Dial-up Network (VPDN), is used to provide users or employees with remote access to a company's network. This setup is widely used by companies whose employees need to access the company's resources securely from different locations, like from home or while traveling.

In a Remote Access VPN, each user needs a VPN client installed on their device. This client is responsible for establishing the connection to the VPN gateway on the company's network, and it encrypts and decrypts the data sent through this connection. This ensures that the connection is secure, and the data cannot be intercepted. Remote Access Virtual Private Networks (VPNs) are essential tools for providing secure connections to remote resources, typically classified into two categories: Internet Protocol Security (IPsec) and Secure Sockets Layer (SSL) VPNs.

Traditionally, IPsec-based VPNs were the prevalent choice for ensuring secure, end-to-end encryption of data transferred between networks. These solutions require the installation of a VPN client on the user's device, and their strength lies in creating secure network-level connections suitable for large enterprise environments.

On the other hand, SSL-based VPNs have surged in popularity in recent years due to their flexibility and ease of use. The unique advantage of SSL VPNs is their ability to be accessed directly from any standard web browser, eliminating the need for a separate VPN client to be installed on the user's device. This makes them more adaptable for various devices, platforms, and user requirements, and thus they have become increasingly favored for individual and small to medium-sized business use.

VPN Protocols

Virtual Private Networks (VPNs) use protocols that encapsulate and encrypt data for secure transmission over internet connections. The different VPN protocols vary in complexity, speed, security level, and ease of setup. We'll discuss the primary ones here: Point-to-Point Tunneling Protocol (PPTP), Layer 2 Tunneling Protocol (L2TP) with Internet Protocol Security (IPsec), Secure Sockets Layer (SSL) and Transport Layer Security (TLS), Internet Key Exchange version 2 (IKEv2), WireGuard, and OpenVPN.

Types of VPN Protocols

PPTP is one of the oldest VPN protocols. It stands out due to its simple setup process and compatibility with most operating systems. However, its simplicity is also its main drawback as it lacks robust security features, making it unsuitable for transmitting sensitive data.

L2TP and IPsec often work together to enhance security in VPN connections. L2TP creates the VPN tunnel, while IPsec ensures data encryption, thereby providing a robust secure connection. However, the enhanced security offered by L2TP/IPsec comes with increased complexity during setup.

SSL and TLS, while primarily used to secure web traffic, can also be used to create VPNs. This implementation enables users to connect to VPNs via their web browsers without the need to install additional software, enhancing user convenience.

IKEv2 is a relatively new entrant in the VPN protocol market. Its main advantage lies in its secure and fast connectivity. It is particularly adept at re-establishing connections if they drop, making it a reliable choice for consistent VPN connections.

WireGuard, another recent VPN protocol, has gained popularity due to its simplicity, speed, and robust security. It has managed to achieve this balance by using a lean codebase, which makes it less susceptible to bugs and security vulnerabilities, making it an attractive choice in the VPN market.

OpenVPN is an open-source VPN protocol known for its robust security and flexibility. Its wide acceptance by many VPN providers can be attributed to its compatibility with a range of encryption algorithms. Operating at the OSI layer 2 or 3, OpenVPN uses SSL/TLS for key exchange, allowing it to effectively navigate network address translators (NATs) and firewalls. This enables peers to authenticate each other through various methods, including pre-shared secret keys, certificates, or username/password combinations.

Explore OpenVPN

The configurations that OpenVPN supports are highly varied. It is compatible with both static key (preshared key) and certificate-based (PKI) setups, and it can operate over UDP or TCP. This adaptability allows OpenVPN to function across various VPN setups, from basic point-to-point links to more complex networks involving multiple machines.

Utilizing the OpenSSL library for encryption, OpenVPN can deploy several cryptographic algorithms, such as 3DES, AES, RC5, and Blowfish. While the default encryption strength is 128-bit, configurations can be adjusted to use up to 256-bit encryption for enhanced security.

A distinct feature of OpenVPN is its resilience in maintaining a VPN connection even when the client's IP address changes. This feature is particularly beneficial for mobile devices transitioning between Wi-Fi networks or shifting from Wi-Fi to mobile data. OpenVPN represents a potent combination of robustness, flexibility, and security among VPN protocols. Its widespread use across personal VPNs and business VPN applications underlines its dependability and versatility in ensuring secure internet connections.

Setting up OpenVPN

For the purpose of this book, we'll focus on how to install and configure OpenVPN on a Linux machine, specifically a Ubuntu distribution. Please ensure you have root (administrator) access to execute these steps.

Update Your System

Before installing any package, it's recommended to update the system's package list. This ensures that you download the latest version of the software. You can do this with the command:

```
sudo apt-get update
```

Install OpenVPN

You can install OpenVPN by typing the following command:

```
sudo apt-get install openvpn
```

Get OpenVPN Configuration File

The configuration file contains details such as the VPN server address and the necessary encryption keys. This file is typically provided by your VPN service provider and should end with the extension .ovpn. Download or move this file into the /etc/openvpn/ directory.

Start OpenVPN Service

To start the VPN connection, use the command sudo openvpn --config followed by the path to your configuration file. For example:

```
sudo openvpn --config /etc/openvpn/myvpn.ovpn
```

This will start OpenVPN and attempt to establish a connection using the settings in the provided configuration file.

Confirm VPN Connection

Once connected, you should see an Initialization Sequence Completed message in the terminal. You can also confirm that your IP address has changed to the VPN server's IP address by visiting an IP-checking website.

Starting OpenVPN on Boot

If you want the VPN to connect automatically when the system starts, you can enable the OpenVPN service to start on boot. First, you need to rename the OpenVPN configuration file to default.conf:

```
sudo mv /etc/openvpn/myvpn.ovpn /etc/openvpn/default.conf
```

Then, enable the OpenVPN service:

```
sudo systemctl enable openvpn@default.service
```

From now on, the VPN will automatically connect when the system starts.

Implementing Site-to-Site VPN

Implementing a Site-to-Site VPN with C++ is quite a complex task. C++ itself does not provide any built-in libraries for creating VPNs. In a typical real-world setup, a network engineer would use specific network equipment or software solutions that support VPN capabilities (such as OpenVPN or WireGuard).

However, to provide an idea of how one might interact with a Site-to-Site VPN programmatically, let us consider the following steps. In this case, we will use an external program to set up the VPN and then use C++ to interface with this program.

Step 1:
We'll assume the use of OpenVPN. To set up OpenVPN for a Site-to-Site VPN, you'll first need to configure the server and client configuration files appropriately on the respective

machines.

Step 2:
Once the VPN is set up, we can use C++ to interact with the VPN. This could involve checking the status of the VPN, sending data over the VPN, or interacting with the VPN software in other ways.

Below is a simplified demonstration of how one might interact with OpenVPN from a C++ program:

```
#include <cstdlib>

int main() {
    // Assume openvpn is in the system path
    // Replace "config.ovpn" with the path to your OpenVPN configuration file
    int result = system("openvpn config.ovpn");

    if (result == 0) {
        std::cout << "VPN connection successful." << std::endl;
    } else {
        std::cout << "Failed to connect VPN." << std::endl;
    }

    return 0;
}
```

In this code, we're calling the system() function, which is a simple way to run an external program from a C++ program. We're running the openvpn command with our configuration file as an argument.

This code will attempt to connect the VPN when run. If the VPN connection is successful, it prints "VPN connection successful." Otherwise, it prints "Failed to connect VPN."

Implementing Remote Access VPN

As stated earlier, creating a VPN is generally not performed with programming languages like C++. Instead, networking professionals use specialized VPN software or appliances from vendors that have their custom libraries and APIs. These APIs are usually written in a higher-level language such as Python, JavaScript, or Ruby.

However, suppose you wish to integrate VPN usage within a C++ application or script. In that case, one way would be to use the system command to control VPN connection software, like OpenVPN, via the command line.

Step 1:
As stated earlier in previous implementation, you need to install and configure OpenVPN on the system where the C++ application will be running. You will need to obtain a VPN profile from your VPN provider, which contains the necessary connection and encryption settings.

Step 2:
After that, we can write a simple C++ program that uses the system() function to control the VPN via OpenVPN's command-line interface:

```
#include <cstdlib>
#include <iostream>

int main() {
    // The command to start the VPN. Replace "myvpn.ovpn" with the path to
your VPN profile.
    std::string startVPNCommand = "openvpn --config myvpn.ovpn --daemon";

    // The command to stop the VPN.
    std::string stopVPNCommand = "killall openvpn";

    // Start the VPN.
    int result = system(startVPNCommand.c_str());

    if (result == 0) {
        std::cout << "VPN connection successful." << std::endl;
    } else {
        std::cout << "Failed to connect VPN." << std::endl;
```

```
        return 1;
    }

    // ... Perform actions while VPN is active ...

    // Stop the VPN.
    result = system(stopVPNCommand.c_str());

    if (result == 0) {
        std::cout << "VPN disconnect successful." << std::endl;
    } else {
        std::cout << "Failed to disconnect VPN." << std::endl;
    }

    return 0;
}
```

This code starts a VPN connection using OpenVPN's command-line interface, then stops the VPN connection when you're done.

Summary

In this chapter, we delved into the world of Virtual Private Networks (VPNs), providing an exhaustive exploration of their importance, functionality, and use cases in modern business environments. We started with the concept of VPNs, highlighting their rise as a critical tool for maintaining privacy and security in an increasingly interconnected digital world. We delved into the technical aspects, explaining how VPNs function by encrypting and encapsulating data for secure transmission over public networks. We discussed the components of a VPN, including the client software, VPN server, and VPN gateway, emphasizing how each part contributes to the overall security and effectiveness of a VPN connection.

We explored the two major types of VPNs: Site-to-Site VPNs and Remote Access VPNs, shedding light on their unique functions and use cases. With Site-to-Site VPNs, we learned how they provide a secure bridge between two or more distinct networks, often located in different geographic locations. The practical aspect was covered by demonstrating interactions with Site-to-Site VPNs using C++. On the other hand, we discussed how Remote Access VPNs allow individual users to connect to a remote network securely as if they were physically present, a feature essential in the era of remote work. We proceeded to practically demonstrate the interaction with Remote Access VPNs using C++.

The chapter culminated with a comprehensive discussion of VPN protocols, focusing on OpenVPN due to its balance of security and performance. We learned about the features that make OpenVPN an excellent choice for many applications, such as its ability to traverse Network Address Translation (NAT) and firewalls, and its support for various encryption algorithms. Moreover, we explored a step-by-step practical walkthrough on installing and configuring OpenVPN on a Linux machine, emphasizing the hands-on skills necessary for effective VPN management. As we close this chapter, we are equipped with a profound understanding of VPNs and the practical knowledge of interacting with them using C++, a skillset critical for any network administrator in the current digital landscape.

CHAPTER 6: WIRELESS NETWORKS

Introduction to Wireless Networks

This chapter embarks on an exciting journey through the realm of wireless networking - a technology that has undeniably revolutionized our connectivity options and significantly changed the way we access and share information. With the advent of wireless networking, the dependency on physical cables for data transmission has reduced remarkably, providing us with the freedom to stay connected, regardless of our location.

Wireless networking functions by transmitting data through electromagnetic waves such as radio frequencies or infrared light. This transmission is governed by a set of rules or protocols, which define the specific ways data should be transmitted and received. The two most commonly used protocols in wireless networking are the Wi-Fi (Wireless Fidelity) and Bluetooth. Wi-Fi is a high-speed wireless networking protocol based on the 802.11 IEEE network standard. It provides internet connectivity to devices like smartphones, computers, and smart appliances within a certain range. Bluetooth, on the other hand, is primarily used for connecting peripheral devices like wireless headphones, mice, and keyboards to a computer within a relatively shorter range. The ubiquitous nature of wireless networks demands stringent security measures. Different wireless security standards have been developed to protect the networks and their users from potential threats. The Wired Equivalent Privacy (WEP) was the first security protocol introduced for wireless networks, but due to its vulnerabilities, it was soon replaced by Wi-Fi Protected Access (WPA). WPA offered a higher level of security than WEP, but it was not perfect. Hence, a more secure protocol, WPA2, was introduced. WPA3, the latest protocol, further improves security by providing robust protections even when users choose weak passwords.

Wireless networking has significantly impacted many areas, including homes, businesses, and public spaces, by providing internet access without the hassle of wiring. It has facilitated the rise of IoT (Internet of Things) devices, empowering smart homes and smart cities, and has played a pivotal role in the growth of mobile devices. However, the convenience of wireless networking comes with its own set of challenges, including security concerns, range limitations, and interference issues.

In the forthcoming topics of this chapter, we will dive deeper into the intricacies of wireless networks, unravel the protocols in detail, explore the security standards thoroughly, and understand how C++ can be utilized for managing and manipulating wireless networks.

Wireless Fidelity (WiFi)

WiFi, or Wireless Fidelity, has become a ubiquitous technology powering our modern world's connectivity. Its architecture is built around a simple yet effective model that allows devices to connect wirelessly to a network, typically the internet, within a certain range. The primary components of a WiFi network are Wireless Access Points (WAPs), Wireless Network Interface Cards (WNICs), and a network infrastructure, which typically involves routers and switches.

The Wireless Access Point, or WAP, is a device that serves as the central transmitter and receiver of wireless signals. It communicates with the Wireless Network Interface Cards (WNICs) present in devices like laptops, smartphones, and tablets. The WAP is typically connected to a wired network, often the internet, and bridges the gap between the wireless devices and the internet. WiFi operates by using radio waves to transmit and receive data. The data to be sent is first transformed into a radio signal by the WNIC in the sending device. This signal is transmitted over the air and received by the WAP, which decodes the radio signal back into data and sends it across the wired network. The process also works in reverse for incoming data.

Regarding the use of C++ for WiFi setup and administration, there are several libraries that can facilitate these tasks. Libraries such as WinPcap and WpdPack for Windows, or libpcap for Linux, can be used for capturing and sending network packets, thus allowing the analysis and manipulation of WiFi traffic. For instance, an administrator can use C++ to create a network scanner, which can discover all devices connected to a WiFi network. This can be achieved by sending probe requests and then capturing and analyzing the probe responses to retrieve information about the connected devices. Also, WiFi security can be programmed and tested using C++, by setting up authentication and encryption mechanisms for network communication. For instance, using cryptographic libraries in C++, a network administrator could implement protocols like WPA2 or WPA3 in a custom network setup.

Note that these tasks require an understanding of lower-level network protocols, and the use of C++ for these purposes is not as straightforward as with high-level languages such as Python. However, C++ offers great performance benefits and the ability to work at a low level with network interfaces, which can be useful for advanced network administration and cybersecurity tasks. In the following chapters, we'll dive deeper into these aspects of C++ network programming.

WiFi Programming using C++

Given the operating system restrictions and the complexities involved in directly interacting with WiFi hardware using C++, it's often a better practice to use high-level libraries, APIs or command-line tools for such tasks, and then integrate these with your C++ program using system calls or process execution. Let us look at an example of how you can use C++ to execute command-line instructions for managing WiFi networks on a Linux system.

The "iw" command-line utility is commonly used in Linux to manage wireless devices and their configuration. You can execute commands from within your C++ program using the system() function, which is available in the cstdlib library. Below is an example of scanning for WiFi networks using this method:

```
#include <cstdlib>

int main() {
   system("iw wlan0 scan | less");
   return 0;
}
```

In the above code, the system() function executes the command-line command "iw wlan0 scan | less". This command lists all available WiFi networks.

If you want to connect to a WiFi network, you may use NetworkManager's nmcli command-line tool, which can also be called from within a C++ program. For example:

```
#include <cstdlib>

int main() {
   system("nmcli dev wifi connect MySSID password MyPassword");
   return 0;
}
```

In the above code, replace MySSID with your WiFi network's SSID and MyPassword with your WiFi password. This command attempts to connect to the specified WiFi network. When you are running these programs, they need to be run with administrator privileges to access network hardware. This can be done by using the sudo command when running your program in the terminal. For a more comprehensive and lower-level manipulation of WiFi networks using C++, you would typically need to use platform-specific APIs.

Bluetooth

Bluetooth is a short-range wireless communication technology that operates in the 2.4 GHz Industrial, Scientific, and Medical (ISM) frequency band. Its primary purpose is to enable wireless data transfer between devices, typically over relatively short distances of up to 100 meters. Bluetooth technology is standardized and maintained by the Bluetooth Special Interest Group (SIG), which consists of several large technology companies. The Bluetooth SIG has developed and released multiple versions of the Bluetooth standard, with each new version introducing improved speed, range, and functionality.

The architecture of Bluetooth involves several layers, including the radio layer, baseband layer, link manager, host controller interface (HCI), logical link control and adaptation protocol (L2CAP), and the application layer.

- Radio Layer: This layer defines the requirements for the radio frequency (RF) and power level used in Bluetooth devices.

- Baseband Layer: This layer manages physical channels and links apart from other services like error correction, data whitening, hop selection, and Bluetooth Security.

- Link Manager: The Link Manager discovers other remote Link Managers and communicates with them via the Link Manager Protocol (LMP), setting up service-level connections.

- Host Controller Interface (HCI): This layer provides a command interface to the baseband controller and link manager.

- L2CAP Layer: This layer multiplexes data between different higher-layer protocols and offers segmentation and reassembly of packets.

- Application Layer: This layer includes various protocols and interfaces, such as RFCOMM, SDP, and others, that provide services to the application software.

Bluetooth is used in enterprises for a variety of purposes, including file sharing, device pairing (such as with wireless keyboards, mice, or headsets), real-time location services, and Internet of Things (IoT) device communication. Bluetooth's low energy requirement (in Bluetooth Low Energy, BLE) makes it suitable for battery-powered IoT devices. However, there are security considerations associated with Bluetooth use in an enterprise setting. Unauthorized devices could potentially connect to an open Bluetooth network, leading to potential data breaches. As a result, careful control of Bluetooth usage is required, with necessary security measures such as device authentication, authorization, and data encryption.

Regarding C++, while there aren't many widely-used libraries available for Bluetooth programming, you could use platform-specific APIs to work with Bluetooth. For instance, on Linux, you could use the BlueZ library, which provides support for the core Bluetooth layers and protocols. On Windows, you would use the Windows.Devices.Bluetooth namespace in the Windows Runtime API.

In the next sections, we'll explore how to use these tools for Bluetooth programming in a C++ environment.

Bluetooth Programming with BlueZ

To interact with Bluetooth devices using C++ on a Linux platform, you'd typically use the BlueZ library. BlueZ is the official Bluetooth protocol stack for Linux and includes support for core Bluetooth layers and protocols. Below is a brief example of how you might use BlueZ to discover nearby Bluetooth devices:

First, install the BlueZ library and its development files with the following command:

```
sudo apt-get install libbluetooth-dev
```

Once you have the BlueZ library installed, you can start using it in your C++ programs. Below is a simple example:

```
#include <iostream>
#include <bluetooth/bluetooth.h>
#include <bluetooth/hci.h>
#include <bluetooth/hci_lib.h>

int main(int argc, char **argv) {
  int dev_id = hci_get_route(NULL);
  int sock = hci_open_dev(dev_id);

  if (dev_id < 0 || sock < 0) {
    perror("Opening socket");
    exit(1);
  }

  inquiry_info *ii = new inquiry_info[255];
  int max_rsp = 255;
```

```
    int num_rsp = hci_inquiry(dev_id, 8, max_rsp, NULL, &ii,
IREQ_CACHE_FLUSH);

    if (num_rsp < 0) {
        perror("Inquiry");
        exit(1);
    }

    for (int i = 0; i < num_rsp; i++) {
        char addr[19] = { 0 };
        ba2str(&(ii + i)->bdaddr, addr);
        std::cout << "Found Bluetooth device: " << addr << std::endl;
    }

    delete[] ii;
    close(sock);

    return 0;
}
```

This example does a Bluetooth device inquiry and prints the addresses of the found devices. Note that this code needs to be run as root to have the necessary privileges to interact with the Bluetooth devices. To do that, you'd compile it with g++ and then run the resulting program with sudo, like so:

```
g++ -o scan scan.cpp -lbluetooth
sudo ./scan
```

This example gives you a basic idea of how you can interact with Bluetooth devices using BlueZ and C++. More complex operations such as pairing with devices, setting up connections, sending and receiving data, etc., would require a deeper dive into the BlueZ API and likely a more structured approach to your program design.

Zigbee

Zigbee is a high-level communication protocol used to create personal area networks built from small, low-power digital radios. Zigbee is often used in applications that require a low data rate, long battery life, and secure networking. It is based on an IEEE 802.15 standard.

The Zigbee architecture consists of three types of devices: Zigbee Coordinator (ZC), Zigbee Router (ZR), and Zigbee End Device (ZED).

1) Zigbee Coordinator (ZC): There is precisely one coordinator in each network which is responsible for initiating the network. The coordinator stores information about the network, including acting as the Trust Center & repository for security keys.

2) Zigbee Router (ZR): The routers can pass on data from other devices. A ZR device has the same functionalities as ZED plus the capability to route data from other devices.

3) Zigbee End Device (ZED): These are devices that connect to the network but do not route packets. They can communicate with the coordinator and routers, depending on the network configuration.

The Zigbee protocol focuses on creating networks with low data traffic, and low power consumption is vital. Zigbee networks are secured with 128-bit symmetric encryption keys, providing a high level of security against unauthorized access and control. In the context of C++ programming, the interaction with Zigbee devices is typically performed via a Zigbee to USB or serial adapter, such as the ones produced by Digi (formerly Digi International). The API provided by such adapters can be used in a C++ program to interact with the Zigbee network.

Zigbee Programming using C++

You can interact with Zigbee devices by using system-level programming in C++ to communicate with a Zigbee module attached via a serial port, by sending and receiving the appropriate commands as defined by the Zigbee communication protocol.

Below is a simplified demonstration of how you might open a serial port in C++ on a Linux system:

```
#include <fcntl.h>
```

```
#include <termios.h>
#include <unistd.h>

int main() {
   int fileDescriptor = open("/dev/ttyUSB0", O_RDWR | O_NOCTTY |
O_SYNC);

   if (fileDescriptor < 0) {
      perror("Error opening serial port");
      return 1;
   }

   struct termios tty = {0};

   if (tcgetattr(fileDescriptor, &tty) < 0) {
      perror("Error from tcgetattr");
      return 1;
   }

   // Set up the tty device attributes here...

   if (tcsetattr(fileDescriptor, TCSANOW, &tty) < 0) {
      perror("Error from tcsetattr");
      return 1;
   }

   // Now the serial port is ready for reading and writing.

   close(fileDescriptor);

   return 0;
}
```

In the above sample program, /dev/ttyUSB0 is the file corresponding to a USB serial port. The open function is used to open this file and obtain a file descriptor, which can then be used to read from and write to the port. The tcgetattr and tcsetattr functions are used to get and set the terminal attributes, respectively. Note that you'd have to fill in the appropriate terminal attribute settings for your specific Zigbee module.

Once the serial port is set up, you can then use the read and write functions to send and receive data. The exact data to send will depend on the commands you wish to send to the Zigbee devices on the network. These commands are defined by the Zigbee specification and often vary between manufacturers, so you'd need to consult the documentation for your specific Zigbee devices to determine the correct command structures.

Wireless Standards: 802.11a/b/g/n/ac/ax

The IEEE 802.11 family, or Wi-Fi, is pivotal to modern wireless networking. As a network administrator, understanding the varying 802.11 standards is crucial as they offer distinct capabilities. Wireless networking has evolved over the years, with standards established by the Institute of Electrical and Electronics Engineers (IEEE) under the 802.11 series, each offering improvements in speed, range, and efficiency. These standards include 802.11a, 802.11b, 802.11g, 802.11n (Wi-Fi 4), 802.11ac (Wi-Fi 5), and 802.11ax (Wi-Fi 6). Variants such as 802.11n, 802.11ac, and 802.11ax (Wi-Fi 6) differ in data rate, range, and bandwidth. These factors must be considered when choosing a standard for specific applications, such as indoor, outdoor, residential, or commercial use, to ensure optimal network performance and user satisfaction.

802.11a

802.11a was among the first wireless standards, operating at a 5 GHz frequency. It can deliver data rates up to 54 Mbps. Its choice of frequency makes it less susceptible to interference compared to standards operating on 2.4 GHz. However, the higher frequency also means a shorter range, which can limit its use in certain applications or environments.

802.11b

The 802.11b standard operates on a 2.4 GHz frequency, providing a slower data rate of up to 11 Mbps. The advantage of this standard is its longer range compared to 5 GHz standards. Yet, the lower frequency band is more crowded and susceptible to interference from other devices such as microwaves and Bluetooth devices.

802.11g

The 802.11g standard, also using the 2.4 GHz frequency, improved on 802.11b's speed by offering data rates up to 54 Mbps. This increase in speed made it a more desirable option for many users, while it still maintained a good range due to its operating frequency.

802.11n (Wi-Fi 4)

The 802.11n standard, also known as Wi-Fi 4, made significant advancements in wireless networking. It operates on both 2.4 GHz and 5 GHz bands and introduced the use of multiple antennas to increase data rates up to a significant 600 Mbps. It was the first standard to incorporate Multiple Input Multiple Output (MIMO) technology, enhancing signal quality and coverage.

802.11ac (Wi-Fi 5)

802.11ac, or Wi-Fi 5, further improved upon the preceding standards. Operating exclusively in the less congested 5 GHz band, it boosted data rates up to a staggering 1.3 Gbps. One of its significant innovations was the introduction of multi-user MIMO (MU-MIMO), a technology allowing multiple users to communicate with the router simultaneously, improving overall network efficiency.

802.11ax (Wi-Fi 6)

The 802.11ax standard, or Wi-Fi 6, is the latest of these standards and is a considerable leap forward in wireless technology, offering data rates up to an impressive 10 Gbps. Wi-Fi 6 operates in both 2.4 GHz and 5 GHz bands and brings significant improvements in handling network congestion. It also enhances the capabilities of MU-MIMO technology, allowing for more efficient transmission and reception of data between multiple devices.

As a network administrator, the key things you should be aware of include:

- Interference: The 2.4 GHz band is commonly used by many devices (including microwaves and Bluetooth devices), which can cause interference. The 5 GHz band is less crowded but has a shorter range.

- Compatibility: Ensure that both your wireless access point and client devices support the same standards. Older devices might not support newer standards like 802.11ac and 802.11ax.

- Throughput vs. Range: Higher frequency standards (like 802.11a and 802.11ac) offer more speed but have a shorter range. Lower frequency standards (like 802.11b and 802.11g) offer less speed but a wider range.

- Environment: The best standard to use depends on the environment. In congested areas with many wireless networks, a 5 GHz band would work best, while in areas with fewer networks, a 2.4 GHz band may suffice.

- Device Density: Newer standards like 802.11ax are designed to handle a high number of devices simultaneously, making them suitable for environments with a high device density.

- Security: Ensure that whatever standard is in use, it supports the latest wireless security protocols. As of my knowledge cutoff, WPA3 is the newest and most secure.

In terms of C++ interaction with wireless standards, the direct low-level handling of these protocols isn't typically done in C++ or any high-level language. Instead, this handling is usually performed by the drivers of the wireless devices, which communicate with the operating system's networking stack. However, as a network administrator, you may need to configure wireless networks or interact with wireless devices from a C++ application. This could involve tasks like scanning for available networks, connecting to a network, configuring network parameters, or transmitting and receiving data over the network. For such tasks, there are several libraries available, like Boost.Asio for general networking tasks, which includes support for sockets and other network primitives. On Linux, you may also use the NetworkManager API via D-Bus for tasks like scanning for available networks or connecting to a network.

Also, understanding these wireless standards is vital when troubleshooting issues in a wireless network. As a network administrator, you would need to understand the nuances of these standards to diagnose and rectify issues. You'd need to identify and eliminate sources of interference, select the most appropriate channels, and optimize your network topology for the best performance.

Finally, you need to understand the security implications of these standards. Older standards like WEP have known vulnerabilities and should not be used. WPA2 or WPA3 should be used instead. You also need to be aware of other security best practices, such as using strong network passwords, disabling SSID broadcasting if necessary, and setting up a guest network for visitors.

Wireless Security Standards

Wireless security is a critical aspect of managing a network, especially given the inherent vulnerabilities of transmitting data through the air. A broad understanding of wireless security standards is, therefore, a must for any network administrator. Below is an in-depth look at the most common wireless security protocols:

Wired Equivalent Privacy (WEP)

Wireless Equivalent Privacy (WEP) is a security protocol for wireless networks, marking a significant initial effort to protect Wi-Fi communications. Using the RC4 stream cipher, WEP provided encryption through 40-bit and 104-bit keys. Despite being an early security measure for Wi-Fi connections, WEP was beset with considerable vulnerabilities.

The main flaw in WEP lies in its encryption implementation. It permits packets to be captured over the network. Once enough data is collected, nefarious individuals can crack the encryption, revealing the network key. This vulnerability isn't a minor hiccup but rather an inherent flaw in the WEP protocol's design. Given the ease with which its encryption can be cracked, WEP doesn't provide reliable security for Wi-Fi networks. Due to these vulnerabilities, WEP is widely recognized as insecure and is generally not recommended for use in safeguarding wireless networks. Instead, newer and more secure protocols like WPA2 or WPA3 should be utilized.

Wi-Fi Protected Access (WPA)

Wi-Fi Protected Access (WPA) was established as an interim solution to remedy the deficiencies of the Wired Equivalent Privacy (WEP) security protocol. WPA retained the use of the RC4 stream cipher, just like WEP, but introduced several robust features that significantly bolstered its security performance. A key component of WPA is the Temporal Key Integrity Protocol (TKIP), a sophisticated mechanism that dynamically changes the encryption key for each data packet transmitted. This feature makes it more difficult for attackers to compromise the encryption, thereby addressing the key static vulnerability that WEP suffered from, which led to its downfall.

Despite the improvements WPA brought over WEP, it's important to note that WPA, particularly when utilizing TKIP, is not devoid of vulnerabilities. As a result, it's now viewed as insecure in the cybersecurity community, highlighting the necessity for the development and implementation of more secure protocols such as WPA2 and WPA3 in wireless networks.

WPA2

Wi-Fi Protected Access 2 (WPA2) represents a major advancement in Wi-Fi security protocols over its predecessor, WPA. It introduced the Advanced Encryption Standard

(AES), a robust encryption algorithm, replacing the Temporal Key Integrity Protocol (TKIP), which was a significant vulnerability in the WPA protocol.

AES provides significantly improved security by using more complex encryption keys and multiple rounds of encryption. It's recognized globally as a highly secure encryption standard, trusted for securing sensitive data, even in governmental systems. Alongside AES, WPA2 also incorporated the Counter Mode Cipher Block Chaining Message Authentication Code Protocol (CCMP). This is a powerful method of authentication that ensures the data's integrity and the sender's identity, providing an additional layer of security.

In a well-implemented scenario, WPA2 remains secure and is considered the standard for secure Wi-Fi connections. The introduction of WPA2 marked a considerable leap in providing secure and reliable Wi-Fi connectivity, setting a high benchmark for subsequent protocols.

WPA3

Wi-Fi Protected Access 3 (WPA3) is the most advanced wireless network security standard. It brings several important enhancements over its predecessor, WPA2, making it harder for attackers to break into a network. One key feature is Simultaneous Authentication of Equals (SAE), a robust method of initial key exchange between devices. SAE guards against so-called "dictionary" attacks, where an attacker systematically tries all possible passwords. In WPA3, even if an attacker captures data from your network, they cannot use it to guess your password.

WPA3 also increases the minimum encryption requirements, delivering a significantly more secure 192-bit security encryption for networks transmitting sensitive data. This level of encryption makes it exceedingly difficult for hackers to decipher intercepted data, ensuring that confidential information remains private and secure. These features combine to make WPA3 a significant step forward in securing Wi-Fi networks, protecting against potential threats, and safeguarding sensitive data transmission.

A network administrator should be well-versed in these wireless security standards, their strengths and weaknesses, and how to implement them effectively in various network environments.

General Practices for Programming Wireless Networks

Programming a wireless network using C++ involves interaction with the Network Interface Card (NIC) and the networking stack of the operating system. On a Linux platform, we usually use system and networking libraries such as NetworkManager and WPA Supplicant. But for this demonstration, let us focus on the 'iw' command for simple tasks and use system calls in C++.

Below are some general steps for working with wireless networks from a C++ application on a Linux platform:

Scan Available Networks

First, we will create a simple C++ program to execute a shell command using system calls and fetch the output. Let us take an example of scanning for available networks. You could use the 'iw' command for this.

```
#include <iostream>
#include <cstdlib> // system, NULL, EXIT_FAILURE

int main()
{
   int result = system("iw dev wlan0 scan | grep SSID");

   if (result != EXIT_SUCCESS)
   {
      std::cerr << "Command execution failed!" << std::endl;
   }

   return 0;
}
```

This program runs the command **iw dev wlan0 scan | grep SSID** which scans for available networks and prints the SSID of each network.

Connecting to Network

In order to connect to a wireless network, you'll typically use a tool like NetworkManager or WPA Supplicant. For instance, to connect to a network using WPA Supplicant, you would create a configuration file with the network's SSID and pre-shared key, and then run the wpa_supplicant command to connect. This is typically done at the shell level rather than directly from a C++ program.

Error Handling

To handle the errors, you may need to catch exceptions and handle the failure of the system calls.

```
#include <iostream>
#include <cstdlib> // system, NULL, EXIT_FAILURE

int main()
{
   int result = system("iw dev wlan0 scan | grep SSID");

   if (result == -1)
   {
      std::cerr << "Failed to execute command!" << std::endl;
   }
   else if (WEXITSTATUS(result) != EXIT_SUCCESS)
   {
      std::cerr << "Command execution failed!" << std::endl;
   }

   return 0;
}
```

In the above program, we are checking if the system call is successful or not. If it's not successful, we are printing an error message.

Sample Program on Querying Wireless Connection

Let us try on the demonstration as above wherein we are querying the connection status of a wireless network.

For this demonstration, we will use the iw command again to check the status of our wireless interface. This program will run the iw dev wlan0 link command, which shows the connection status.

```
#include <iostream>
#include <cstdlib>
#include <array>
#include <memory>

std::string exec(const char* cmd) {
    std::array<char, 128> buffer;
    std::string result;
    std::unique_ptr<FILE, decltype(&pclose)> pipe(popen(cmd, "r"), pclose);
    if (!pipe) {
        throw std::runtime_error("popen() failed!");
    }
    while (fgets(buffer.data(), buffer.size(), pipe.get()) != nullptr) {
        result += buffer.data();
    }
    return result;
}

int main()
{
    std::string cmd = "iw dev wlan0 link";
    std::string output = exec(cmd.c_str());

    std::cout << "Command output: " << std::endl;
    std::cout << output << std::endl;
```

```
    return 0;
}
```

In the above sample program, we've created an exec function that executes a command and returns its output as a std::string. The popen function opens a pipe to a process that's created by running the given command in a shell. It returns a file stream that can be used to read the output of the command.

The fgets function reads data from the pipe into the buffer, and this is appended to the result string.

Finally, the main function runs the iw dev wlan0 link command and prints its output.

Summary

This chapter gave an insightful and practical exploration of wireless networking, starting with a comprehensive understanding of the wireless network landscape. The foundation was laid by offering an overview of wireless networks, their evolution, the architecture, and the various protocols at play. This set the stage for understanding the different types of wireless communication technologies prevalent in modern enterprises such as WiFi, Bluetooth, and Zigbee.

We dug deep into each technology, starting with WiFi, learning its architecture and how C++ can be used for setting up and administering WiFi networks. Following a similar structure, we dove into Bluetooth technology, its architecture, use-cases, and finally a hands-on demonstration of Bluetooth programming using C++. Zigbee, an exciting low-power, low-cost, wireless mesh networking technology, also followed the same pattern of theory followed by practical coding demonstrations.

The chapter then transitioned to the finer details of wireless networking standards and wireless security standards that every network administrator should be familiar with. We discussed the spectrum of 802.11 standards, their peculiarities, and what makes them distinct. The importance of wireless security was stressed upon as we delved into the various security standards such as WEP, WPA, WPA2, and WPA3. Finally, we put all these concepts to practice by using C++ to perform various wireless network operations like setting up the network, network configuration, scanning networks, and connecting to networks on a Linux platform. Through this chapter, we illustrated how one could leverage C++ to interact with the wireless network environment, bringing an element of programming agility into network administration tasks.

CHAPTER 7: ASYNCHRONOUS PROGRAMMING

Getting Started with Asynchronous Programming

What is Asynchronous Programming?

Asynchronous programming, in its simplest terms, is a form of programming that allows multiple operations or tasks to be processed concurrently but not necessarily simultaneously. This approach is a significant departure from synchronous or blocking I/O programming where tasks are executed in sequence, one task blocking the next until it completes. In network operations, responsiveness and efficiency are critical. Given that many network tasks involve waiting for I/O operations (like reading from or writing to a network socket), using a synchronous approach might not be the best use of resources. This is where asynchronous programming comes in. With asynchronous programming, while a task is waiting for an I/O operation to complete, the CPU can be utilized to perform other tasks.

For example, consider a server handling multiple client requests. In a synchronous model, the server would handle each client request one after the other, making other clients wait if one client is slow or a particular operation takes longer than expected. However, in an asynchronous model, the server can initiate a request, then move on to start processing another request even before the first request has completed. Once the first request completes, the server can then go back and finish processing it. Asynchronous programming, thus, provides a way to build more efficient, responsive and scalable network applications. It's especially useful for tasks that are I/O-bound, such as network operations, where you often have to wait for data to be sent or received over the network. With asynchronous operations, your program can continue to execute other code while waiting for these I/O operations to complete.

The C++offers several libraries and constructs to perform asynchronous operations. These include the Standard C++ Library, Boost.Asio, and others. By properly leveraging these tools, you can write network programs in C++ that efficiently handle multiple simultaneous connections, improving the scalability and performance of your applications. This chapter will dive deep into the intricacies of asynchronous programming, specifically in the context of networking tasks.

Why not Synchronous Programming?

The difference between synchronous and asynchronous programming is primarily in the way tasks or operations are managed and executed within a program. In synchronous programming, operations are executed in sequence, one after the other. If an operation involves some I/O (like reading from a file or sending data over a network), the entire program halts and waits for the operation to complete. No further execution happens until the current operation is finished. The main advantage of this approach is simplicity; the flow of control is straightforward and easy to understand since it follows a sequential pattern. However, the downside is inefficiency; while the program is waiting for an I/O operation to complete, the CPU remains idle even though it could be doing other useful work.

Asynchronous programming, on the other hand, allows multiple operations to occur concurrently. When an operation that involves I/O is initiated, the program does not wait for it to complete. Instead, it can move on to execute other operations. Once the I/O operation is completed, a callback function is typically invoked to handle the result of the operation. This approach allows for better utilization of resources because the CPU can keep working on other tasks while waiting for I/O operations to complete. It also leads to more responsive programs because they can continue to react to user input even when an I/O-bound operation is in progress. However, asynchronous programming is typically more complex than synchronous programming due to the handling of callbacks and the need to manage the concurrent execution of tasks.

In the context of network programming, synchronous operations would mean a server handles each client request one at a time. In contrast, with asynchronous operations, the server could handle multiple client requests concurrently, thereby potentially serving more clients in the same amount of time. For network-intensive tasks that involve managing multiple connections or tasks concurrently, asynchronous programming can often provide better performance and scalability.

Callbacks, Promises, and Async/Await

When dealing with asynchronous programming, we often use mechanisms like callbacks, futures/promises, and async/await to manage and synchronize concurrent tasks. Below is a brief overview of these concepts:

Callbacks

A callback in programming, particularly in C++, is a powerful tool that enhances software's modularity and functionality. Essentially, a callback is a function you provide to another function as an argument. The callee function then executes this callback function at the appropriate time. This pattern enables a lower-level software layer to invoke a function defined in a higher-level layer, providing a form of inversion of control.

In C++, you implement callbacks using function pointers or functors (function objects).

Function pointers hold the memory address of a function and can be invoked just like regular functions. Functors, on the other hand, are objects that can be treated as though they are a function or function pointer. They are instances of a class that defines the operator() method. Both function pointers and functors serve as effective means for defining and handling callbacks in C++, providing flexibility and enhancing the structure of complex software systems.

Below is a simple example of a callback using a function pointer:

```
void execute(void (*callbackFunc)(int), int value) {
    callbackFunc(value);
}

void printValue(int value) {
    std::cout << "Value: " << value << std::endl;
}

int main() {
    execute(printValue, 5);
    return 0;
}
```

In the above sample program, printValue function is the callback that gets called inside the execute function.

Futures and Promises

Promises and futures in the C++ Standard Library are fundamental components for managing asynchronous operations, particularly in multi-threaded programming. A promise object, in essence, is a data structure that holds some type of value, not immediately available, but will be computed or retrieved at a later time. This value is then accessed by an associated future object.

The future object, on the other hand, provides a mechanism to access the result from a promise. It 'waits' for the promise to fulfill and provides the promised value. The significant aspect is that futures ensure proper synchronization when the promise and future objects are accessed from different threads, preventing any data race conditions. This mechanism of promises and futures makes it easier to write concurrent code, ensuring safe and synchronized communication between threads in C++.

Below is a simple example of a promise and future:

```
#include <future>
#include <iostream>

void calculate(std::promise<int> intPromise) {
   intPromise.set_value(10);  // Fulfill promise (this happens in a different thread)
}

int main() {
   std::promise<int> prom;
   std::future<int> fut = prom.get_future();
   std::thread t(calculate, std::move(prom));
   std::cout << fut.get() << std::endl;  // Get result (potentially in yet another
thread)
   t.join();
   return 0;
}
```

In the above sample program, the calculate function promises to provide a value which is then retrieved by fut.get().

Async/Await

C++, unlike languages such as JavaScript or Python, doesn't inherently support the async/await syntax. Despite this, you can implement asynchronous functionality via its Standard Library features, specifically std::async and std::future. The std::async function template in C++ allows you to initiate an asynchronous task. This function will operate independently of the main thread and execute a specified task concurrently.

Meanwhile, std::future is a feature in the C++ Standard Library that retrieves the value from an asynchronous task. It represents a future (yet-to-be-computed) value, allowing the result of the std::async operation to be accessed when it's ready. This combination of std::async and std::future offers a comparable, though arguably more complex, mechanism to the async/await syntax found in other programming languages. This enables developers to write asynchronous code in C++, taking advantage of concurrent execution for enhanced application performance.

Below is an example:

```
#include <future>
#include <iostream>

int calculate() {
   return 10;
}

int main() {
   std::future<int> fut = std::async(calculate);
   std::cout << fut.get() << std::endl;
   return 0;
}
```

In the above sample program, the calculate function is executed asynchronously and its return value can be retrieved with fut.get(). This mimics the functionality of async/await found in other languages.

Writing Asynchronous using Callbacks

Let us create a simple server-client model using Boost.Asio library to illustrate these concepts. We'll be using the async functions provided by Boost.Asio which allow us to write asynchronous code in a simpler way.

Below is an example of a simple echo server that uses callbacks.

```
#include <boost/asio.hpp>
#include <iostream>

using boost::asio::ip::tcp;

class Session : public std::enable_shared_from_this<Session> {
```

```
public:
  Session(tcp::socket socket) : socket_(std::move(socket)) {}

  void Start() {
    DoRead();
  }

private:
  void DoRead() {
    auto self(shared_from_this());
    socket_.async_read_some(boost::asio::buffer(data_, max_length),
      [this, self](boost::system::error_code ec, std::size_t length) {
        if (!ec) {
          DoWrite(length);
        }
      });
  }

  void DoWrite(std::size_t length) {
    auto self(shared_from_this());
    boost::asio::async_write(socket_, boost::asio::buffer(data_, length),
      [this, self](boost::system::error_code ec, std::size_t /*length*/) {
        if (!ec) {
          DoRead();
        }
      });
  }

  tcp::socket socket_;
  enum { max_length = 1024 };
  char data_[max_length];
};
```

```
class Server {
public:
  Server(boost::asio::io_context& io_context, short port)
    : acceptor_(io_context, tcp::endpoint(tcp::v4(), port)) {
    DoAccept();
  }

private:
  void DoAccept() {
    acceptor_.async_accept(
      [this](boost::system::error_code ec, tcp::socket socket) {
        if (!ec) {
          std::make_shared<Session>(std::move(socket))->Start();
        }
        DoAccept();
      });
  }

  tcp::acceptor acceptor_;
};

int main(int argc, char* argv[]) {
  try {
    boost::asio::io_context io_context;
    Server s(io_context, std::atoi(argv[1]));
    io_context.run();
  } catch (std::exception& e) {
    std::cerr << "Exception: " << e.what() << "\n";
  }
  return 0;
}
```

This example uses the Boost.Asio library's asynchronous API. The async_read_some and async_write functions are non-blocking and take callbacks (lambdas in this case) as parameters. These callbacks will be invoked when the operations complete.

Multithreading and Concurrency

Multithreading and concurrency are fundamental concepts in C++ for writing efficient, fast, and responsive applications.

Exploring Multithreading

Multithreading is a type of execution model where multiple threads are spawned by the main program (process) to execute different tasks concurrently in the same shared memory space. Each thread operates independently and can execute different tasks simultaneously. The operating system divides processing time not only among different applications but also among each thread within an application.

Understanding Concurrency

Concurrency in programming is a key concept that relates to the execution of tasks. Specifically, it pertains to the ability of a system to manage multiple tasks simultaneously. However, the term 'simultaneously' may be misleading. In concurrency, tasks don't necessarily execute in strict parallel fashion. Instead, they start, run, and complete in overlapping time intervals. This could mean that a single task is broken down into sub-tasks which are executed independently, or multiple tasks are interweaved, giving an illusion of simultaneous execution. This mechanism enhances the efficiency of a system, improves performance, and optimizes resource utilization, making it a crucial concept in modern computing environments.

C++ provides several tools for multithreading and concurrency:

- std::thread: This is the main class for dealing with threads in C++. You create a new thread and provide a function that the thread should execute.

- std::async & std::future: std::async launches a function asynchronously (potentially in a new thread) and returns a std::future that will eventually hold the result of that function. This is a higher level, often easier-to-use way to manage concurrency.

- std::mutex and std::lock_guard: These are used to protect shared data from concurrent access. Mutex stands for "mutual exclusion", and a std::lock_guard is an object that locks a mutex in its constructor and unlocks it in its destructor, providing an easy way to keep a mutex locked for a block of code.

- std::atomic: This class template provides functionality for fine-grained atomic operations, allowing for lock-free programming of concurrent data structures.

- std::condition_variable: This is used to allow threads to communicate with each other by waiting for a condition to become true.

One of the key challenges in multithreading and concurrent programming is ensuring that concurrent operations do not collide and cause data inconsistencies (race conditions). C++ provides several mechanisms for synchronization such as mutexes, locks, condition variables, atomic variables, and memory barriers to ensure safe access to shared data. Learning to effectively use multithreading and concurrency in C++ can help you write applications that are more responsive and take full advantage of today's multi-core processors.

Creating Multi-threaded Server

Implementing multithreading and concurrency for networking in C++ allows us to execute multiple tasks simultaneously and optimize resource usage. In this case, we'll create a simple multi-threaded server that handles multiple client connections simultaneously.

```
#include <iostream>
#include <thread>
#include <boost/asio.hpp>

using boost::asio::ip::tcp;

void session(tcp::socket sock) {
  try {
    char data[1024];
    for (;;) {
      boost::system::error_code error;
      size_t length = sock.read_some(boost::asio::buffer(data), error);
      if (error == boost::asio::error::eof)
        break; // Connection closed cleanly by peer.
      else if (error)
        throw boost::system::system_error(error); // Some other error.
```

```
            boost::asio::write(sock, boost::asio::buffer(data, length));
        }
    }
    catch (std::exception& e) {
        std::cerr << "Exception in thread: " << e.what() << "\n";
    }
}

void server(boost::asio::io_service& io_service, short port) {
    tcp::acceptor a(io_service, tcp::endpoint(tcp::v4(), port));
    for (;;) {
        tcp::socket sock(io_service);
        a.accept(sock);
        std::thread(session, std::move(sock)).detach();
    }
}

int main(int argc, char* argv[]) {
    try {
        boost::asio::io_service io_service;
        server(io_service, std::atoi(argv[1]));
    }
    catch (std::exception& e) {
        std::cerr << "Exception: " << e.what() << "\n";
    }
    return 0;
}
```

This above program uses Boost.Asio and creates a simple echo server that reads data from a client and writes it back. For each new client connection, a new thread is started that runs the session function. This function reads data from the socket and writes it back until the client closes the connection. In this way, the server can handle multiple client connections simultaneously, each on their own thread.

Always make sure to join threads (or detach them as done here) to prevent leaks and undefined behavior. Furthermore, proper exception handling should be implemented to ensure the stability and reliability of the system. Properly utilizing multithreading and concurrency in C++ can greatly improve the efficiency, responsiveness, and throughput of network applications.

Asynchronous I/O and libuv

What is Asynchronous I/O?

Asynchronous I/O, or non-blocking I/O, is a powerful technique that enhances computing efficiency. It works by allowing a program to initiate an I/O operation and then continue with other tasks without waiting for the I/O operation to complete. This ability to multitask is crucial for maintaining application performance and responsiveness, particularly in I/O-intensive applications or services. This approach is a stark contrast to synchronous, or blocking, I/O where a program must pause execution until an I/O operation is completed, which can result in inefficient use of resources and lower application responsiveness. Hence, asynchronous I/O plays a key role in optimizing computing systems and building high-performance applications.

Explore Libuv

libuv is a multi-platform support library with a focus on asynchronous I/O. It was primarily developed for use by Node.js, but it's also used by Luvit, Julia, pyuv, and others. It's a powerful library that provides the core I/O functionality for Node.js and is known for its performance and efficiency. It exposes interfaces for TCP, UDP, timers, filesystem operations, signal handling, and more, all in an asynchronous fashion.

libuv provides several core features:

- Full-featured event loop backed by epoll, kqueue, IOCP, event ports.
- Asynchronous TCP and UDP sockets
- Asynchronous DNS resolution
- Asynchronous file and file system operations
- File system events
- ANSI escape code controlled TTY
- IPC with socket sharing, using Unix domain sockets or named pipes (Windows)
- Child processes
- Thread pool
- Signal handling

- High resolution clock
- Threading and synchronization primitives

libuv also provides the user with a set of utility functions and it is written in C, making it a library that is not only hardy but also lightweight. While libuv is not a C++ library and does not provide a C++ interface, C++ programs can use it directly through its C API or use a C++ wrapper library. It is not used as commonly in C++ as Boost.Asio for asynchronous I/O, but it is a very powerful and efficient library used by some of the most demanding software in terms of I/O operations, like Node.js.

Sample Program on Asynchronous I/O

Let us create a simple TCP Echo Server that uses asynchronous I/O operations.

```
#include <iostream>
#include <boost/asio.hpp>

using boost::asio::ip::tcp;

class session
{
public:
  session(boost::asio::io_context& io_context)
    : socket_(io_context)
  {
  }

  tcp::socket& socket()
  {
    return socket_;
  }

  void start()
  {
    socket_.async_read_some(boost::asio::buffer(data_, max_length),
```

```
    boost::bind(&session::handle_read, this,
      boost::asio::placeholders::error,
      boost::asio::placeholders::bytes_transferred));
}

void handle_read(const boost::system::error_code& error,
  size_t bytes_transferred)
{
  if (!error)
  {
    boost::asio::async_write(socket_,
      boost::asio::buffer(data_, bytes_transferred),
      boost::bind(&session::handle_write, this,
        boost::asio::placeholders::error));
  }
  else
  {
    delete this;
  }
}

void handle_write(const boost::system::error_code& error)
{
  if (!error)
  {
    socket_.async_read_some(boost::asio::buffer(data_, max_length),
      boost::bind(&session::handle_read, this,
        boost::asio::placeholders::error,
        boost::asio::placeholders::bytes_transferred));
  }
  else
  {
    delete this;
```

```
    }
  }

private:
  tcp::socket socket_;
  enum { max_length = 1024 };
  char data_[max_length];
};

class server
{
public:
  server(boost::asio::io_context& io_context, short port)
    : io_context_(io_context),
    acceptor_(io_context, tcp::endpoint(tcp::v4(), port))
  {
    start_accept();
  }

  void start_accept()
  {
    session* new_session = new session(io_context_);
    acceptor_.async_accept(new_session->socket(),
      boost::bind(&server::handle_accept, this, new_session,
        boost::asio::placeholders::error));
  }

  void handle_accept(session* new_session,
    const boost::system::error_code& error)
  {
    if (!error)
    {
      new_session->start();
```

```
    }
    else
    {
      delete new_session;
    }

    start_accept();
  }

private:
  boost::asio::io_context& io_context_;
  tcp::acceptor acceptor_;
};

int main(int argc, char* argv[])
{
  try
  {
    if (argc != 2)
    {
      std::cerr << "Usage: async_tcp_echo_server <port>\n";
      return 1;
    }

    boost::asio::io_context io_context;

    using namespace std; // For atoi.
    server s(io_context, atoi(argv[1]));

    io_context.run();
  }
  catch (std::exception& e)
  {
```

```
    std::cerr << "Exception: " << e.what() << "\n";
  }

  return 0;
}
```

The server accepts connections and starts a session for each one. A session is a series of reads and writes to and from the connected client. When a read completes, the data read is written back to the client; when the write completes, another read is initiated. This sequence of operations continues until an error occurs (such as the client closing the connection), at which point the session is destroyed.

This sample program demonstrates using asynchronous I/O to handle multiple clients at the same time with a single thread..

Sample Program on TCP Echo Server using libuv

A simple TCP echo server using libuv would look like this:

```
#include <stdio.h>
#include <stdlib.h>
#include <string.h>
#include <uv.h>

#define DEFAULT_PORT 7000
#define DEFAULT_BACKLOG 128

void alloc_buffer(uv_handle_t *handle, size_t suggested_size, uv_buf_t *buf) {
  buf->base = (char*) malloc(suggested_size);
  buf->len = suggested_size;
}

void echo_write(uv_write_t *req, int status) {
```

```
  if (status) {
    fprintf(stderr, "Write error: %s\n", uv_strerror(status));
  }
  char *base = (char*) req->data;
  free(base);
  free(req);
}

void echo_read(uv_stream_t *client, ssize_t nread, const uv_buf_t *buf) {
  if (nread < 0) {
    if (nread != UV_EOF)
      fprintf(stderr, "Read error: %s\n", uv_err_name(nread));
    uv_close((uv_handle_t*) client, NULL);
  } else if (nread > 0) {
    uv_write_t *req = (uv_write_t *) malloc(sizeof(uv_write_t));
    req->data = (void*) buf->base;
    uv_buf_t wrbuf = uv_buf_init(buf->base, nread);
    uv_write(req, client, &wrbuf, 1, echo_write);
  }

  if (buf->base)
    free(buf->base);
}

void on_new_connection(uv_stream_t *server, int status) {
  if (status < 0) {
    fprintf(stderr, "New connection error: %s\n", uv_strerror(status));
    return;
  }

  uv_tcp_t *client = (uv_tcp_t*) malloc(sizeof(uv_tcp_t));
  uv_tcp_init(uv_default_loop(), client);
  if (uv_accept(server, (uv_stream_t*) client) == 0) {
```

```
        uv_read_start((uv_stream_t*) client, alloc_buffer, echo_read);
    } else {
        uv_close((uv_handle_t*) client, NULL);
    }
}

int main() {
    uv_tcp_t server;
    uv_tcp_init(uv_default_loop(), &server);

    struct sockaddr_in addr;
    uv_ip4_addr("0.0.0.0", DEFAULT_PORT, &addr);

    uv_tcp_bind(&server, (const struct sockaddr*)&addr, 0);

    int r = uv_listen((uv_stream_t*) &server, DEFAULT_BACKLOG,
on_new_connection);
    if (r) {
        fprintf(stderr, "Listen error: %s\n", uv_strerror(r));
        return 1;
    }
    return uv_run(uv_default_loop(), UV_RUN_DEFAULT);
}
```

This code starts a server on port 7000 and echos back whatever data is sent to it.

Summary

This chapter unraveled the world of asynchronous programming in the context of C++ networking. As the first step, we dug deep into the concept of asynchronous programming and how it differentiates from synchronous programming, emphasizing the immense benefits it offers in terms of non-blocking operations and better resource utilization.

In our journey, we discovered the intricate mechanisms of Callbacks, Promises, and async/await in C++. With detailed walkthroughs and practical demonstrations, we learned to effectively implement these in networking tasks. Further, we unveiled the concepts of

Multithreading and Concurrency in C++, which opened doors to improved efficiency in networking by executing multiple threads and tasks concurrently. Again, practical demonstrations made it clear how to harness these powerful features in our networking programs.

The last part of the chapter introduced the 'libuv' library that supports asynchronous I/O. We saw how 'libuv' is used in creating a simple TCP echo server, thus showing its practicality in networking operations. It's clear that mastering asynchronous programming, along with multithreading and concurrency, are keys to creating robust, efficient, and responsive networking applications with C++. Our exploration into asynchronous programming with C++ has not only equipped us with essential networking skills but also broadened our understanding of C++ as a powerful language for network programming.

CHAPTER 8: NETWORK TESTING AND SIMULATION

Overview

This chapter introduces you to the imperative and often understated realm of network testing and network simulations. In today's complex networking environments, it's crucial to evaluate the performance, reliability, and security of network systems. This is where network testing and simulation play their role. Network testing methodologies allow us to ensure that the network is performing optimally, and the services are being delivered as expected. They can validate the functionality of individual network components and the system as a whole, identify potential bottlenecks, and help develop strategies to mitigate them. The methodologies range from stress testing, where the network is pushed beyond its normal operational capacity, to security testing, which focuses on identifying vulnerabilities that can be exploited by attackers.

Additionally, the chapter also underscores the role of network simulations, which involve creating a model of the network and then running simulations to predict how it will behave under various conditions. Network simulations can be highly beneficial when planning for network expansion, or when considering the introduction of new protocols or services. The C++ language provides various libraries for network testing and simulation. Libraries like Network Simulator 3 (NS-3), OMNeT++, and SimGrid can help to model, simulate, and analyze the performance of networks. These libraries offer an extensive range of features, from simple packet-level simulations to more complex network scenarios involving numerous nodes and various protocols.

In the modern networking arena, the role of network testing and simulation can't be overstated. They form an integral part of the network design, planning, and management processes. As network administrators, having proficiency in network testing and simulation methodologies and being able to leverage C++ libraries for this purpose, can enable us to maintain high-performing and secure networks. This chapter aims to instill this understanding and equip you with practical skills in network testing and simulations using C++.

Network Testing Methodologies

Network testing methodologies are crucial to maintaining a healthy, efficient, and secure network. There are several methodologies, each focusing on a specific aspect of the network's operation. Let us delve into a few of these:

1) Functional Testing: This type of testing aims to confirm that the individual components of the network are functioning as expected. In practice, this could involve using C++ to write scripts that perform automated testing on routers, switches, or firewalls to ensure they are functioning correctly.

2) Performance Testing: This methodology focuses on evaluating the speed, reliability, and capacity of the network under various loads and stress conditions. This could involve writing C++ programs that generate network traffic and measure the response times, throughput, and error rates.

3) Stress Testing: Stress testing, a subset of performance testing, pushes the network beyond its normal operational capacity to identify bottlenecks and points of failure. This can involve writing C++ code to simulate large volumes of traffic, connections, or data transfers.

4) Security Testing: Security testing aims to identify vulnerabilities that could be exploited by attackers. This could involve writing C++ scripts to simulate attacks on the network, such as DDoS attacks or penetration testing.

5) Load Testing: Load testing is another subset of performance testing, which focuses on understanding the network's behavior under a specific expected load. This load could be the maximum number of users that the network can support simultaneously or any other criterion as per the network requirements.

6) Compatibility Testing: This testing ensures that the network is compatible across different devices, platforms, operating systems, or network configurations. You can write C++ programs to test if your network can run on different devices or systems efficiently.

Network administrators use C++ and its libraries to automate many of these testing processes. For example, using socket programming, you can write scripts to simulate network traffic for load or stress testing. Libraries such as Boost.Asio is helpful in writing asynchronous network operations, critical for simulating real-world network scenarios. The goal of network testing is not just to identify problems but to anticipate and mitigate them.

Functional Testing

Functional testing is a type of testing that validates whether individual components of the network are functioning as expected. In networking terms, this could include various elements like routers, switches, firewalls, access points, network interfaces, and software-defined networking (SDN) components.

The objective of functional testing is to ensure that all the elements within the network setup perform their expected tasks without any issues. This encompasses checking the correct data packet forwarding, ensuring proper load balancing, validating efficient routing protocols operation, and verifying successful network connections.

Step-by-Step

This type of testing typically involves several stages, including identifying the functions to be tested, creating input data, determining expected outputs, executing tests, and reviewing the results. It's an essential part of maintaining network health, security, and efficiency, and should form part of any comprehensive network management strategy. To effectively carry out functional testing in a network environment, the following steps are typically taken:

Identify the Functions to be Tested

Firstly, it is critical to identify the specific network components or functions to be tested. These might be various hardware devices within the network, such as routers, switches, or servers, or they could be certain software functionalities within network applications or protocols. The precise scope of testing will depend on the network's complexity, its size, and the specific requirements of the organization.

Create Input Data

The next stage involves creating suitable input data for the testing process. This data will be used to simulate a variety of network conditions and interactions with the chosen components or functions. It is important that the input data is as realistic and comprehensive as possible to adequately test the network's capabilities and performance under different conditions.

Determine Expected Outputs

After preparing the input data, the expected outputs for each test case need to be determined. This essentially means defining what the 'correct' result should be when the input data is processed by the component or function being tested. This step is crucial as it forms the benchmark against which the actual outcomes of the tests can be compared to determine whether they have passed or failed.

Execute Tests

The testing process itself involves executing the tests using the prepared input data. This might involve using specialized network testing tools or writing code, such as in C++, to feed the input data into the functions under test and then capture and analyze the outputs. Any discrepancies between the expected and actual outcomes must be carefully documented and investigated.

Review and Retest

The final stage of functional testing is to review the results and, where necessary, retest components or functions after any issues have been rectified. This process may need to be repeated several times until all the tested network functions behave as expected under all test conditions.

Conduct Functional Testing using PcapPlus

Below is an example using C++ and the PcapPlusPlus library for testing a network packet handling function:

```
#include "PcapPlusPlus/IPv4Layer.h"
#include "PcapPlusPlus/Packet.h"

bool testPacketHandling() {
    // Create a mock IP packet
    pcpp::IPv4Layer ipLayer(pcpp::IPv4Address("1.1.1.1"),
pcpp::IPv4Address("2.2.2.2"));
    pcpp::Packet packet;
    packet.addLayer(&ipLayer);

    // Expected output: the packet's total length
    uint16_t expectedOutput = ipLayer.getHeaderLen();

    // Call the function to be tested: get the packet's total length
    uint16_t actualOutput = packet.getRawPacket()->getRawDataLen();

    // Compare actual output with expected output
    if (actualOutput != expectedOutput) {
        return false;  // Test failed
    }
    return true;  // Test passed
}

int main() {
    bool result = testPacketHandling();
```

```
    if (result) {
        std::cout << "Test passed!\n";
    } else {
        std::cout << "Test failed!\n";
    }
    return 0;
}
```

This example illustrates the process of creating mock data (an IP packet), determining the expected output (the packet's total length), calling a function to retrieve the actual output (using the packet's getRawDataLen() method), and comparing the actual output with the expected output to verify if the test passed or failed. This fundamental testing process can be extrapolated to more complex network scenarios and functions.

In real-world scenarios, the testing would be much more comprehensive, covering various network protocols, hardware, and configurations but this example demonstrates the overall functional testing concept.

Performance Testing

Performance testing in the context of networking aims to measure the speed, reliability, and capacity of a network. This type of testing can identify network bottlenecks, measure throughput, and assess the overall network quality under various traffic conditions. Performance testing often focuses on high-load scenarios and seeks to determine at what point the system's performance degrades or fails.

The primary types of performance testing are:

1) Load Testing: Verifies the system's behavior under normal and peak conditions.
2) Stress Testing: Checks system behavior under conditions beyond its capacity.
3) Endurance Testing: Examines the system under a significant load for an extended period.
4) Spike Testing: Assesses the system's response to sudden, significant changes in load.

Step-by-Step

Performance testing is a crucial part of system development and maintenance that ensures the system can handle intended loads effectively. It involves several steps, from understanding the system to analyzing test results. Below is a high-level description of the steps involved in performance testing:

Understand the System

The initial step in performance testing is gaining an in-depth understanding of the system. Familiarize yourself with the system's structure, its performance-critical components, and their interactions. Components may include routers, firewalls, network interfaces, servers, databases, etc. Recognize the system's boundaries and limitations, such as bandwidth and storage capacity. This foundational knowledge is essential for identifying potential bottlenecks and planning your tests effectively.

Identify Performance Metrics

The next step is to identify the performance metrics that will be tracked throughout the testing process. These are measurable aspects that give insight into the system's performance. In a network environment, this could be metrics like response time, throughput (amount of data moved successfully from one place to another in a given time period), network latency (delay in data communication over the network), packet loss rate (percentage of packets that fail to reach their destination), or error rate. The choice of metrics depends on the system's nature and the goals of performance testing.

Plan and Design Performance Tests

Following the identification of metrics, the next phase is planning and designing performance tests. You need to determine the type of performance testing necessary, depending on your system's requirements and your performance objectives. This could include load testing (how the system behaves under an expected load), stress testing (how it behaves under extreme load), endurance testing (how it behaves over a long period of load), or spike testing (how it handles sudden, significant increases in load). Define the load or request rate for these tests and select suitable tools to generate this load and measure the resulting performance metrics.

Execute Tests

The fourth step is executing the designed tests. This step could vary significantly based on your testing environment and tools. For instance, in the case of C++, this might involve writing and running scripts that simulate network traffic, create high-load scenarios, and measure performance metrics.

Analyze Results

Finally, after completing the tests, it's time to analyze the results. During this stage, the collected data is reviewed to identify any performance bottlenecks, inconsistencies, or other areas that require improvement. You'll need to correlate these findings with your initial performance metrics and expectations. If any performance issues are found, you'll need to drill down to their root causes, devise potential solutions, and test those solutions.

Performance testing is a cyclic process. The system should be re-tested after any changes, ensuring continued performance efficiency. By following these steps, you can ensure your system is robust and ready to meet the demands of your users.

Conduct Performance Testing on TCP Server

Below is a simplified demonstration of how one might conduct a performance test on a TCP server using the Boost.Asio library:

```
#include <boost/asio.hpp>
#include <iostream>
#include <chrono>

int main() {
    boost::asio::io_service io_service;

    // Connect to the server
    boost::asio::ip::tcp::socket socket(io_service);
    socket.connect(boost::asio::ip::tcp::endpoint(
        boost::asio::ip::address::from_string("127.0.0.1"), 1234));

    // Record the start time
    auto start = std::chrono::steady_clock::now();

    // Send data to the server
    for (int i = 0; i < 10000; ++i) {
        std::string message = "Hello, server!";
        boost::asio::write(socket, boost::asio::buffer(message));
    }

    // Record the end time
```

```
    auto end = std::chrono::steady_clock::now();

    // Calculate the elapsed time
    std::chrono::duration<double> elapsed_seconds = end - start;
    std::cout << "Elapsed time: " << elapsed_seconds.count() << "s\n";

    return 0;
}
```

In this code, a TCP client connects to a local server and sends a series of messages. We record the time before and after the message sending process to calculate how long it takes. The time taken can be an important performance metric, indicating how quickly the server can handle incoming messages. The more extensive the test (e.g., sending larger amounts of data or over longer periods), the more accurately it can simulate real-world usage and provide meaningful performance data.

Stress Testing

Stress testing evaluates a network's robustness and error handling capabilities under extreme conditions. It can reveal many issues in the network, such as memory leaks, synchronization issues, and many others. The test pushes the network beyond its normal operation capacity to determine the breaking point or limit.

Consider a case where you want to stress test a TCP server. The goal might be to find out how many simultaneous connections the server can handle. You can use Boost.Asio library in C++ to simulate thousands of clients connecting and sending messages to the server simultaneously. You will monitor the performance metrics of your interest, such as response time, CPU usage, and memory consumption. In network stress testing, you need to keep in mind that this process can and usually does degrade the performance of the system under test and can even result in a temporary system failure.

Perform Network Stress Testing

Below is an example of how to perform a stress test on a server by simulating multiple concurrent connections:

```
#include <boost/asio.hpp>
#include <vector>
```

```
int main() {
    boost::asio::io_service io_service;
    std::vector<boost::asio::ip::tcp::socket> sockets;

    // Attempt to open 10000 connections to the server
    for (int i = 0; i < 10000; ++i) {
        sockets.emplace_back(io_service);
        sockets.back().connect(boost::asio::ip::tcp::endpoint(
            boost::asio::ip::address::from_string("127.0.0.1"), 1234));
    }

    // Hold the connections open
    std::this_thread::sleep_for(std::chrono::minutes(1));

    return 0;
}
```

This simple script tries to create 10,000 simultaneous connections to a server running on localhost. It holds the connections open for one minute. During this time, you can monitor the server's performance and behavior. Does it successfully accept all connections? Does its response time increase? How much CPU and memory does it use?

These are practical examples and may need to be adapted based on the actual testing framework and network settings you are using. This example gives a strong understanding of how one might approach performance testing of network applications using C++.

Security Testing

Security testing is another crucial network testing methodology. The primary aim is to uncover vulnerabilities, threats, risks in a network that could lead to loss of information, data theft, and other potential damage that might violate the network's security policies.

In C++, several libraries can assist with security testing, one of which is "libtins". Libtins is a high-level, multiplatform C++ network packet sniffing and crafting library. It's designed to allow the construction, parsing, and sending of network packets. With libtins, you can analyze packet data, sniff live packets, or even create new ones from scratch.

Using ARP for Security Testing

Let us say you want to scan your network to find all devices connected to it. You can use the Address Resolution Protocol (ARP) request method to accomplish this.

```
#include <tins/tins.h>
#include <map>
#include <iostream>

using namespace Tins;
using namespace std;

map<IPv4Address, HWAddress<6>> ips;

bool callback(const PDU& pdu) {
   const ARP &arp = pdu.rfind_pdu<ARP>();
   ips[arp.sender_ip_addr()] = arp.sender_hw_addr();
   return true;
}

int main() {
   SnifferConfiguration config;
   config.set_promisc_mode(true);
   config.set_filter("arp");
   Sniffer sniffer("eth0", config);
   sniffer.sniff_loop(callback);
   for (const auto &entry : ips) {
      cout << entry.first << " - " << entry.second << endl;
   }
}
```

In this code, we first set up a sniffer that listens for ARP packets on the "eth0" interface.

We store each unique IP-MAC pair we encounter and print them at the end. This security testing technique can reveal all devices on your network. This example provides a starting point for understanding network testing methodologies.

Network Simulations

Overview

Network simulations are indeed an essential asset for network administrators. They enable the creation of a virtual model of a network, replicating its functionality, and allowing exploration of different scenarios and conditions. Simulations provide valuable insights into a network's behavior, predicting how it might respond under various circumstances, from minor traffic fluctuations to major infrastructure changes.

Utilizing network simulations can prevent making direct modifications to a live network, which could be expensive and potentially interrupt essential services. It offers a safe environment to test new configurations, software, or hardware, and measure their impact on network performance before actual implementation. Moreover, they can aid in capacity planning, allowing administrators to assess how the network would cope with increased data volume or additional users.

In essence, network simulations promote proactive network management, improving decision-making, minimizing risks, and leading to more efficient and reliable network operations. They act as a "sandbox," providing a testing ground for experimentation and learning without endangering the actual network.

Benefits

Network simulations play a vital role in managing and optimizing network systems. They offer several benefits, including predicting network behavior, planning upgrades, testing new technologies, and staff training.

One significant advantage of network simulations is the ability to anticipate network behavior under different traffic loads or configurations. It provides insights into how the network might respond under varying conditions, helping identify potential bottlenecks or issues and optimize the network performance.

Furthermore, simulations aid in the planning of network upgrades and expansions. By assessing the impact of changes before implementation, administrators can make informed decisions, minimizing disruptions and ensuring efficient utilization of resources.

Testing new technologies or configurations in a risk-free environment is another benefit of network simulations. This allows administrators to understand the potential effects and tweak configurations without impacting the live network, thereby reducing risks associated with network changes.

Network simulations also serve as a valuable training tool for network administrators and other IT staff. By creating various network scenarios, simulations offer practical learning experiences in dealing with network issues, contributing to skill development and problem-solving efficiency.

In C++, NS-3 is a widely-used library for network simulations. Predominantly used in research and development, NS-3 allows users to create network nodes, connect them with different network devices, assign IP addresses, and simulate packet transfers. This ability to emulate complex network environments makes NS-3 a powerful tool for studying network behavior and enhancing network systems.

Performing Network Simulations

For example, suppose you're creating a network simulation with two nodes. Below is how you might do it:

```
#include "ns3/core-module.h"
#include "ns3/network-module.h"
#include "ns3/internet-module.h"
#include "ns3/point-to-point-module.h"
#include "ns3/applications-module.h"

using namespace ns3;

int main () {
  NodeContainer nodes;
  nodes.Create (2);

  PointToPointHelper pointToPoint;
  pointToPoint.SetDeviceAttribute ("DataRate", StringValue ("5Mbps"));
  pointToPoint.SetChannelAttribute ("Delay", StringValue ("2ms"));
```

```
 NetDeviceContainer devices;
 devices = pointToPoint.Install (nodes);

 InternetStackHelper stack;
 stack.Install (nodes);

 Ipv4AddressHelper address;
 address.SetBase ("10.1.1.0", "255.255.255.0");

 Ipv4InterfaceContainer interfaces = address.Assign (devices);

 UdpEchoServerHelper echoServer (9);

 ApplicationContainer serverApps = echoServer.Install (nodes.Get (1));
 serverApps.Start (Seconds (1.0));
 serverApps.Stop (Seconds (10.0));

 UdpEchoClientHelper echoClient (interfaces.GetAddress (1), 9);
 echoClient.SetAttribute ("MaxPackets", UintegerValue (1));
 echoClient.SetAttribute ("Interval", TimeValue (Seconds (1.0)));
 echoClient.SetAttribute ("PacketSize", UintegerValue (1024));

 ApplicationContainer clientApps = echoClient.Install (nodes.Get (0));
 clientApps.Start (Seconds (2.0));
 clientApps.Stop (Seconds (10.0));

 Simulator::Run ();
 Simulator::Destroy ();

 return 0;
}
```

This is an easy example of a C++ network simulation using NS-3. In this simulation, two nodes are created and connected via a point-to-point link. The second node is set up as a UDP echo server, while the first node is set up as a client that sends a UDP packet to the server. The simulation then runs, and the packet's journey from client to server is modeled.

In this chapter, you will further explore the possibilities offered by C++ for network simulation, giving you a better understanding of the network's behavior and preparing you for the variety of scenarios you may encounter as a network administrator.

NS-3

NS-3 is an open-source, highly extensible network simulator that provides substantial support for simulation of TCP, routing, and multicast protocols over both wired and wireless (WiFi) networks. The tool is widely used in research and development to evaluate the performance and reliability of network protocols and architectures.

Features of NS-3

Below are some key features and elements of NS-3:

- Discrete-event network simulator: NS-3 simulates the journey of individual packets from source to destination across a network. It models network protocols and reactions to data flow, latency, packet loss, and other network phenomena.

- Detailed network models: NS-3 includes extensive models of existing network protocols and architectures, including TCP/IP, UDP, Ethernet, and WiFi. This makes it an effective tool for designing and testing new network protocols, architectures, or modifications.

- Real-world testing: NS-3 can interface with real-world networks, allowing for "hybrid" simulations where part of the network is simulated and part is a live network. This is valuable for testing new protocols or configurations before implementing them on a live network.

- C++ and Python API: NS-3 provides interfaces for both C++ and Python. This gives you flexibility in designing simulations and allows you to use the language that best suits your needs. For network professionals who work extensively with C++, NS-3 offers an opportunity to leverage their existing skills and knowledge.

- Modules: The functionality in NS-3 is organized into modules. Each module encapsulates a specific area of network functionality or a specific network protocol. For example, there are modules for TCP, UDP, Ethernet, WiFi, Internet routing protocols, and so on.

- Integration with other tools: NS-3 can be integrated with other tools for further analysis. For example, it can generate PCAP files for packet-level analysis in Wireshark. It can also interface with visualization tools for graphical representation of network simulations.

Network Simulation using NS-3

Setting up a network simulation using NS-3 in C++ involves several steps, each representing key aspects of the network model you are trying to recreate. The main purpose of these simulations is to observe and analyze network behavior under different conditions.

Process of Network Simulation

To set up a network simulation using NS-3 in C++, you would typically follow these steps:

Create nodes

First, create the nodes. In NS-3, nodes are entities that can send or receive packets across a network, functioning as end systems or routers. Each node is an abstraction of a computer host in the network, capable of running network protocols.

Create and configure network devices

Secondly, create and configure the network devices. Network devices, such as Wi-Fi devices, Ethernet devices, or point-to-point devices, are linked to nodes. These devices enable the nodes to transmit and receive packets. Depending on the network's complexity you are modeling, each node could have one or multiple network devices.

Create and configure a channel

The third step is to create and configure a channel. Channels in NS-3 simulate the medium through which packets travel, such as wireless radio frequency spectrum or wired cables. The channel you choose depends on the type of network being simulated.

Install the network stack

Next, you'll need to install the network stack on each node. The network stack includes the protocols that enable network communication, such as Internet Protocol (IP), Transmission Control Protocol (TCP), or User Datagram Protocol (UDP). These protocol stacks dictate how data is sent and received across the network.

Assign IP addresses

Once the network stack is installed, assign unique IP addresses to each network device. This process is similar to how devices on an actual network are assigned unique identifiers to facilitate communication.

Create and install applications

Finally, create and install applications on the nodes. Applications in NS-3 generate network traffic, simulating the real-world data that flows over the network. Examples could include a simple ping application that sends ICMP echo requests, or more complex applications simulating voice over IP or video streaming.

NS-3 simulations are very flexible and can range from simple examples with just a few nodes to complex simulations of large networks with hundreds or thousands of nodes. By providing a controlled, reproducible environment for network experiments, NS-3 is a valuable tool for network professionals and researchers.

Setting up Network Simulation using NS-3

Let us simulate a simple network with two nodes connected by a point-to-point link.

Install NS-3

Before we begin, ensure that NS-3 is installed on your system. You can download it from the official NS-3 website and follow the installation instructions for your specific operating system.

Create a new simulation script

Create a new C++ file for your simulation. Let us call it simple-network.cc. This script will be where we configure our network and run our simulation.

Include necessary header files

We need to include the necessary NS-3 header files. For our simple simulation, we'll need the following:

```
#include "ns3/core-module.h"
#include "ns3/network-module.h"
#include "ns3/internet-module.h"
#include "ns3/point-to-point-module.h"
```

```
#include "ns3/applications-module.h"
```

Set up the main function

All NS-3 simulations start with a main function, which looks like this:

```
int main (int argc, char *argv[])
{
  // Simulation code here

  return 0;
}
```

Create nodes

Create two nodes and install the Internet stack on them:

```
ns3::NodeContainer nodes;
nodes.Create (2);

ns3::InternetStackHelper stack;
stack.Install (nodes);
```

Create a point-to-point link

We'll connect our nodes using a point-to-point link:

```
ns3::PointToPointHelper pointToPoint;
pointToPoint.SetDeviceAttribute ("DataRate", StringValue ("5Mbps"));
pointToPoint.SetChannelAttribute ("Delay", StringValue ("2ms"));

NetDeviceContainer devices;
devices = pointToPoint.Install (nodes);
```

Assign IP addresses

We'll assign IP addresses to the nodes:

```
ns3::Ipv4AddressHelper address;
address.SetBase ("10.1.1.0", "255.255.255.0");

ns3::Ipv4InterfaceContainer interfaces = address.Assign (devices);
```

Set up applications

Let us set up a simple UDP echo server and client. The server will be on the first node, and the client on the second:

```
UdpEchoServerHelper echoServer (9);

ApplicationContainer serverApps = echoServer.Install (nodes.Get (0));
serverApps.Start (Seconds (1.0));
serverApps.Stop (Seconds (10.0));

UdpEchoClientHelper echoClient (interfaces.GetAddress (0), 9);
echoClient.SetAttribute ("MaxPackets", UintegerValue (1));
echoClient.SetAttribute ("Interval", TimeValue (Seconds (1.0)));
echoClient.SetAttribute ("PacketSize", UintegerValue (1024));

ApplicationContainer clientApps = echoClient.Install (nodes.Get (1));
clientApps.Start (Seconds (2.0));
clientApps.Stop (Seconds (10.0));
```

Run the simulation

Finally, we run the simulation:

```
ns3::Simulator::Run ();
ns3::Simulator::Destroy ();
```

Build and run

To build and run your simulation, use the ./waf command in the NS-3 directory:

```
./waf --run simple-network
```

And we are done. This is easily doable network simulation with two nodes communicating over a point-to-point link. The NS-3 framework is incredibly flexible and powerful, and you can create far more complex simulations by adding more nodes, different types of links, different applications, and much more.

Summary

This chapter dove into the realm of network testing and simulation, critical tools in the network administrator's arsenal for ensuring the reliability, efficiency, and robustness of network systems. We began with an overview of network testing methodologies and the essential role they play in maintaining the health of our networks. We further identified how using C++ libraries contributes to network performance enhancement, stress testing, and security testing.

We discussed and practically demonstrated two crucial testing methodologies: Functional and Performance testing. We learned how Functional Testing ensures the correct operation of the network's individual components, providing a robust foundation. Performance Testing, on the other hand, evaluates the network's efficiency under various loads and conditions, providing insights for optimization. We learned how to apply these methods practically, using tools and techniques available in C++.

Lastly, we ventured into network simulations, tools to replicate the functioning of network systems. We explored NS-3, a discrete-event network simulator, widely regarded for its efficiency and flexibility in modeling various network scenarios. We dissected its architecture, getting a grip on how it works, and then practically set up a network simulation using NS-3 and C++. From setting up nodes to assigning IP addresses and applications, we stepped through the entire process, equipping ourselves to build and understand even more complex network simulations in the future. This chapter was a crucial stepping stone, equipping us with the practical knowledge to assess, diagnose, and improve network systems.

CHAPTER 9: NETWORK CONFIGURATION MANAGEMENT

Network Configurations Overview

This chapter takes us into the fascinating world of Network Configuration Management. Network configuration refers to the detailed setup of a network -- the nuts and bolts that define how a network operates. This encompasses both the hardware and software components of a network system, from IP addresses, DNS settings, and protocols used, to firewall configurations, and router/switch setups. The way these settings and devices interact establishes the performance, security, and reliability of a network.

Different types of network configurations exist, such as Peer-to-Peer (P2P) where each node has the same responsibilities and Client-Server where nodes are either servers providing services or clients using them. Hybrid, a combination of two or more topologies, is another type. The type of network configuration chosen depends on factors such as the organization's size, the network's purpose, and budget constraints. Now, maintaining and managing these configurations is an integral part of a network administrator's duties. Network Configuration Management is the process of organizing and controlling the configurations of all network devices in a systematic way. It involves tasks like tracking & documenting changes made to the network, ensuring that the system is running the correct configurations, and reverting changes if problems occur.

Network Configuration Management is crucial for several reasons. Firstly, it improves the efficiency of the network by ensuring optimal configuration settings. Secondly, it enhances network security by controlling changes and preventing unauthorized modifications. Finally, it aids in troubleshooting by offering visibility into the network's settings and their modifications over time.

When it comes to C++, network configuration management becomes more powerful and efficient. C++ provides robust and extensive libraries that can be utilized to manipulate network configurations, automate tasks, and monitor changes. The standard and networking libraries offer features to work with sockets, protocols, and manage I/O operations, while other libraries such as Boost.Asio provide higher-level abstractions for asynchronous programming, which is crucial in maintaining responsive network services.

In the following topics, we'll explore how we can perform network configuration management tasks using C++ and its libraries, effectively employing C++ as a tool to enhance our network's performance, security, and reliability.

Network Configuration Protocol (NETCONF)

What is NETCONF?

NETCONF (Network Configuration Protocol) is a network management protocol developed and standardized by the Internet Engineering Task Force (IETF). It provides mechanisms to install, manipulate, and delete the configuration of network devices, all communicated via Remote Procedure Call (RPC) methods. Its operations are carried out on a data model that precisely defines the configuration and state data manipulated by the protocol.

NETCONF offers several notable features. Firstly, it supports configuration datastores, enabling separate copies of the device's configuration for operational running and planned configurations. Secondly, it supports powerful filtering capabilities, allowing the retrieval of specific parts of the configuration data. It also provides capabilities for error detection, network transactions, and locks to prevent simultaneous conflicting configuration changes.

NETCONF typically uses XML encoding, which makes it compatible with various programming languages, including C++. While there's no standard C++ library specifically for NETCONF, C++'s extensive range of libraries and its inherent network programming capabilities allow developers to interact with NETCONF.

The interaction with NETCONF in C++ would typically involve creating a client that can send XML-based RPCs over a transport protocol (usually SSH). Libraries like libxml2 can be used to parse and manipulate XML data, and libssh or similar can be employed to handle the SSH communication.

NETCONF Message

Below is a simple example of what a NETCONF message might look like in code (Note: This is a simplified demonstration, actual implementation would require proper handling of XML and SSH):

```
#include <libxml/parser.h>
#include <libssh/libssh.h>

// Create a new NETCONF message
xmlDocPtr doc = xmlNewDoc(BAD_CAST "1.0");
```

```
xmlNodePtr rpc = xmlNewNode(NULL, BAD_CAST "rpc");
xmlNewProp(rpc, BAD_CAST "message-id", BAD_CAST "101");
xmlDocSetRootElement(doc, rpc);

// Add an operation to the message
xmlNewChild(rpc, NULL, BAD_CAST "get-config", NULL);

// Send the message over SSH using libssh
ssh_session session;
// Setup SSH session here
ssh_channel channel = ssh_channel_new(session);
// Send the XML document as a string over the channel
ssh_channel_write(channel, xmlDocDumpMemory(doc, NULL),
strlen(xmlDocDumpMemory(doc, NULL)));
```

This C++ code creates a new NETCONF RPC message asking for the device's configuration and sends it over an SSH channel. The response would then be read from the SSH channel and parsed back into an XML document for processing.

NETCONF using C++

NETCONF operates on a client-server model where the network device is the server, and the network management system is the client. This communication between the client and the server happens over a reliable, connection-oriented protocol such as SSH. The messages exchanged between the client and the server are encoded in XML and follow a Remote Procedure Call (RPC) paradigm.

This means that a client sends a request to perform a certain operation (an RPC), and the server responds with a reply. Operations in NETCONF include get, edit-config, delete-config, copy-config, lock, and unlock. These commands allow for retrieval, modification, and locking/unlocking of the configuration data.

NETCONF Process

Establishing and managing a NETCONF session over SSH is a multi-step process involving a series of interactions between the client and server. It involves the establishment of an SSH connection, initialization of a NETCONF session, sending of NETCONF requests, processing of responses, and ultimately, session closure. This process is fundamental for network management tasks, enabling the configuration and monitoring of network devices.

Let us break down the process of setting up a NETCONF client using C++.

SSH Connection Establishment

The first phase is establishing the SSH connection. Since most NETCONF implementations use SSH as the transport protocol, setting up an SSH connection forms the base for a NETCONF session. To do this, an SSH library like libssh is used to set up the SSH session, authenticate the client, and open a channel for communication between the client and the server. Authentication can be done using username/password or public key methods.

NETCONF Session Initialization

Following the SSH connection, the next step is initializing the NETCONF session. This involves the exchange of hello messages between the client and server to negotiate NETCONF capabilities. The client sends a hello message containing the NETCONF capabilities it supports, to which the server responds with its own hello message outlining its capabilities. This exchange allows both sides to understand and adapt to each other's capabilities, laying the groundwork for future communication.

Sending NETCONF Requests

With the NETCONF session initiated, the client can begin sending NETCONF requests. These requests are essentially Remote Procedure Call (RPC) messages formatted in XML and sent over the SSH channel. Libraries such as libxml2 can be used to generate these XML messages. These messages could be for various operations like retrieving configuration data, modifying configuration data, or invoking specific operations.

Processing NETCONF Responses

Upon sending a request, the client must then process the corresponding response from the server. This involves reading data from the SSH channel, parsing the XML response, and then processing the results accordingly. This could mean displaying the data to a user, updating a database, triggering further actions, or logging the data for future analysis.

Session Closure

Finally, once the desired operations have been performed, the NETCONF session is closed. The client sends a <close-session> request, which terminates the NETCONF session. It's crucial to close sessions properly to free up resources and maintain network security.

This comprehensive process enables communication between the client and network devices, enabling effective network management. By following these steps, network engineers can interact with and manage their network devices using the NETCONF protocol over SSH, providing for efficient, standardized, and powerful network configuration and management capabilities.

Various Network Configuration Tasks

Network configuration encompasses a wide range of activities, including device setup, security configuration, performance tuning, diagnostics and monitoring, fault management and recovery, software and firmware updates, protocol configuration, and configuration via protocols like Network Configuration Protocol (NETCONF). With programming languages such as C++, you can automate and streamline these processes, making network management more efficient and effective.

Below is a summary of some key operations:

Device Configuration

Device configuration is one of the fundamental tasks in network management. It involves setting up network devices such as routers, switches, firewalls, and other hardware to perform their specific roles in the network. This setup process includes configuring settings like IP addresses, subnet masks, default gateways, VLANs, and other parameters. Using C++, network engineers can directly interact with these devices, using low-level networking APIs and protocols to automate this configuration process. This not only saves time and reduces the chance of manual errors but also allows for consistency across multiple devices.

Security Configuration

Security configuration is another critical aspect. The rise of cyber threats has made network security an imperative part of network management. This involves setting up firewalls, virtual private networks (VPNs), access control lists (ACLs), and other security measures to protect the network from malicious attacks. With C++, you can interface with network security APIs to programmatically configure and control security settings, enhancing the overall network security and reducing the potential for human error.

Performance Tuning

Performance tuning of a network involves configuring various parameters to enhance the network's performance. This includes configuring quality of service (QoS) settings to prioritize certain types of traffic, congestion control algorithms to manage network traffic during peak times, and packet scheduling policies to manage how packets are transmitted over the network. C++ can interact with low-level networking APIs to directly control these settings, allowing for a granular control over network performance.

Diagnostics and Monitoring

Diagnostics and monitoring are vital to maintain the network's health. Running diagnostic tools like ping or traceroute, setting up monitoring solutions to keep track of network performance, and processing the output for further analysis are all part of this. C++ can be used to automate these tasks, reducing the time and effort required for routine network monitoring and diagnostics.

Fault Management and Recovery

Fault management and recovery involve preparing for and dealing with network failures. C++ can be used to write programs that automate this recovery process. For instance, in the event of a network device failure, a C++ program could automatically switch to a backup configuration or restart the failed device, minimizing downtime and ensuring network reliability.

Software and Firmware Updates

Software and firmware updates for network devices are necessary to maintain security and introduce new features or bug fixes. Automating this process using C++ can ensure that all devices in the network are running the latest and most secure software versions, contributing to the overall security and efficiency of the network.

Protocol Configuration

Protocol configuration is an important part of network configuration. It involves setting parameters for various network protocols like TCP/IP, UDP, etc. C++ can be used to directly manipulate these protocol settings, allowing for a highly customized network configuration.

Configuration via NETCONF

Lastly, the Network Configuration Protocol (NETCONF) provides a standardized way to install, manipulate, and delete the configuration of network devices. By creating a NETCONF client using C++, you can automate this process, enabling you to manage network configurations in a standardized, programmatic manner.

Automating Firmware Updates

Before we get started, it is essential to point out that the actual code that is used to automate firmware updates may be different depending on the devices that are being used and the protocols that are supported by those devices. In addition, it is essential to update the device's firmware in a cautious manner because an incorrect update can cause the device to malfunction.

Below is a high-level conceptual example of how you could structure your C++ code:

```
#include <iostream>
#include <string>
#include <fstream>

class NetworkDevice {
public:
    virtual void updateFirmware(std::string filePath) = 0;
};

class Router : public NetworkDevice {
public:
    void updateFirmware(std::string filePath) override {
        // Example: Code to send file to router via FTP/TFTP, and initiate update
        std::cout << "Updating router firmware with file: " << filePath << std::endl;
        // Implement specific code here for your router
    }
};

class Switch : public NetworkDevice {
public:
    void updateFirmware(std::string filePath) override {
```

```
        // Example: Code to send file to switch via SCP/SFTP, and initiate update
        std::cout << "Updating switch firmware with file: " << filePath << std::endl;
        // Implement specific code here for your switch
    }
};

int main() {
    // Check that firmware file exists
    std::string firmwarePath = "/path/to/firmware";
    std::ifstream ifile(firmwarePath);
    if(!ifile) {
        std::cerr << "Firmware file does not exist!" << std::endl;
        return 1;
    }

    Router router;
    Switch switch_device;

    // Initiate firmware updates
    router.updateFirmware(firmwarePath);
    switch_device.updateFirmware(firmwarePath);

    return 0;
}
```

This example assumes that the router and switch are distinct types of network devices that each require different protocols to perform a firmware update. It uses the "updateFirmware" function to encapsulate the behavior of updating firmware, which will differ depending on the specific network device.

The code for actually sending the file to the device and initiating the update isn't provided, because it depends on the specific device and protocol. You might use an FTP library for routers, or an SCP/SFTP library for switches, for instance.

In the main function, we create instances of a Router and Switch and then call their updateFirmware functions. This demonstrates the basic idea of using polymorphism to handle different types of network devices in a generalized way.

Manipulate Settings of TCP and UDP

In C++, you can manage and fine-tune their settings at the socket level. This involves changing various socket options and behaviors, such as adjusting timeout settings, buffer sizes, and setting flags for different modes of operation. By manipulating these options, developers can optimize communication parameters to suit specific needs, enhancing the performance and reliability of network applications.

Below is a simple example:

```
#include <iostream>
#include <sys/socket.h>
#include <netinet/in.h>
#include <netinet/tcp.h>

int main() {
    int sockfd;
    int flag = 1;

    // Create a TCP socket
    sockfd = socket(AF_INET, SOCK_STREAM, 0);
    if (sockfd < 0) {
        std::cerr << "Failed to create socket!" << std::endl;
        return 1;
    }

    // Enable TCP_NODELAY (disables Nagle's algorithm)
    int result = setsockopt(sockfd, IPPROTO_TCP, TCP_NODELAY, &flag,
sizeof(int));
    if (result < 0) {
        std::cerr << "Failed to set TCP_NODELAY!" << std::endl;
```

```
    return 1;
  }

  // Create a UDP socket
  sockfd = socket(AF_INET, SOCK_DGRAM, 0);
  if (sockfd < 0) {
    std::cerr << "Failed to create socket!" << std::endl;
    return 1;
  }

  // Enable SO_BROADCAST (enables sending of broadcast messages)
  result = setsockopt(sockfd, SOL_SOCKET, SO_BROADCAST, &flag,
sizeof(int));
  if (result < 0) {
    std::cerr << "Failed to set SO_BROADCAST!" << std::endl;
    return 1;
  }

  return 0;
}
```

In the above sample program, we're doing two things:

For a TCP socket, we're enabling the TCP_NODELAY option. This option disables Nagle's algorithm, which is a TCP feature that attempts to automatically improve efficiency by buffering small packets and sending them together. Disabling it might improve performance for certain applications that want to send out small packets immediately.

For a UDP socket, we're enabling the SO_BROADCAST option. This allows the socket to send broadcast messages, which are messages that are intended to be received by all devices on the local network.

This is a great example and demonstrates the core idea of how you can adjust the settings of TCP and UDP sockets in C++. In a real application, you would likely have more complex requirements and behaviors, and might need to adjust other socket options as well.

Recovery during Failure

The key to recover to pre-configured settings in the event of a failure lies in maintaining robust backups and utilizing mechanisms that allow for quick restoration of these settings. While C++ in itself doesn't provide any specific tools for backup and recovery, your application can design a methodology to handle this.

Let us consider an example where we maintain a backup of network configurations in a file. We'll use JSON for simplicity.

Store Configuration

Assume we have a file config_backup.json that stores a backup of our configurations:

```
{
  "TCP_NODELAY": true,
  "SO_BROADCAST": false
}
```

Read Configuration

We can use a JSON library (like nlohmann/json) to read this configuration:

```
#include <iostream>
#include <fstream>
#include <nlohmann/json.hpp>

nlohmann::json read_config(const std::string& filename) {
  std::ifstream i(filename);
  nlohmann::json config;
  i >> config;
  return config;
}
```

Apply Configuration

We can use this data to configure our sockets:

```
void apply_config(int sockfd, const nlohmann::json& config) {
    int flag;

    flag = config["TCP_NODELAY"];
    setsockopt(sockfd, IPPROTO_TCP, TCP_NODELAY, &flag, sizeof(int));

    flag = config["SO_BROADCAST"];
    setsockopt(sockfd, SOL_SOCKET, SO_BROADCAST, &flag, sizeof(int));
}
```

Recover from Failure

In the event of a failure, we can revert back to our backup configurations:

```
void recover_from_failure(int sockfd, const std::string& backup_filename) {
    nlohmann::json config = read_config(backup_filename);
    apply_config(sockfd, config);
}
```

This example gives an idea of how you could implement a recovery process and in a real-world scenario, your configuration might contain a lot more settings, and your recovery process might be a lot more complex.

Automate Running Diagnostic Tools

The simplest and quickest way to run diagnostic tools like traceroute and ping in C++ is by using system calls. A system call allows you to run a shell command from within your program.

Before we get into the code, it's important to understand that using system calls can have security implications, as it allows for command injection if the command string is constructed using unsanitized user input. So, use this method judiciously and ensure that user inputs are properly sanitized.

Also, the standard system() function is synchronous, it will block the execution of your program until the command has finished running. If you need to run these commands in the background, or in parallel with your program, you'll need to use more complex methods, like creating a separate thread or using a non-blocking system call.

Below is a simple example of running a ping and a traceroute command using the system call:

```
#include <cstdlib> // for system()

int main() {
    // Run a ping command
    system("ping -c 4 www.google.com");

    // Run a traceroute command
    system("traceroute www.google.com");

    return 0;
}
```

In this code, we're using the system function from the cstdlib library to run shell commands. The "-c 4" option in the ping command tells ping to only send 4 packets before stopping. The commands are given as string arguments to the system function.

When you run this program, it will run the ping command, wait for it to finish, then run the traceroute command, and wait for it to finish. If you need to process the output of these commands in your program, you'll need to redirect the command's output to a file, and then read that file in your program.

Configure Access Control Lists and Firewalls

In a Linux environment, we can use iptables and IP sets to configure access control lists and firewalls. As a network administrator, you can make use of C++ and shell scripting to interact with iptables and IP sets programmatically.

While directly manipulating these configurations through C++ code is complex, you can make use of system() function to run command-line instructions in C++ code. However, please be aware of the security implications when using system() function as it can lead to shell command injection vulnerabilities. Always validate and sanitize input if your command incorporates user or third-party input.

Below is a simple example of how you might add a rule to block incoming traffic from a specific IP address using iptables:

```
#include <cstdlib> // for system()
#include <string>

void blockIP(const std::string& ip) {
    std::string cmd = "iptables -A INPUT -s " + ip + " -j DROP";
    system(cmd.c_str());
}

int main() {
    blockIP("192.168.1.100"); // replace with the IP you want to block
    return 0;
}
```

This program runs the iptables -A INPUT -s <IP> -j DROP command to append a new rule to the INPUT chain to drop all packets from a specified IP address. The blockIP function takes a string argument that specifies the IP address to block. The function constructs the iptables command as a string, then runs it using the system function. In the main function, we call blockIP with the IP address we want to block. When you run this program, it will block all incoming traffic from the specified IP address.

Summary

In this chapter, we delved deep into the world of Network Configuration Management with C++. We started with an understanding of what network configurations are, their types and the critical role of Network Configuration Management in maintaining the smooth operations of a network infrastructure. We learnt about NETCONF, a network management protocol that provides methods to install, manipulate, and delete configurations of network devices and its potential integration with C++.

We then moved onto practical aspects, where we explored how to automate various network operations using C++. This included firmware updates, adjusting TCP/UDP settings, recovering pre-configured settings after failure, running diagnostic tools like traceroute and ping, and configuring Access Control Lists and firewalls (on Linux platform). We discussed the possibility of using system calls in C++ to execute shell commands that allow us to automate these tasks, while keeping in mind the security implications of this approach.

Throughout this chapter, the objective was to empower network professionals with the knowledge to perform network configuration tasks using C++, thereby enhancing the ability to manage networks more efficiently and effectively. From setting up network configurations to recovering from failure scenarios, the lessons learned in this chapter provide a foundation for any network professional to leverage C++ in their day-to-day work.

CHAPTER 10: NETWORK MONITORING

Network Monitoring Overview

Network monitoring is a critical component of modern IT operations. It is the continuous process of observing and checking the status of a computer network with the aim of identifying and addressing issues before they escalate into significant problems. Its importance stems from the need to maintain a high level of network performance, reliability, and security, and it is essential to the effective management of any network, regardless of its size or complexity. Monitoring enables the detection of overloaded or crashed servers, network connections, or other devices. This information allows network administrators to respond swiftly and effectively, often before users even notice an issue. Additionally, it aids in maintaining up-to-date network documentation, tracking system usage and capacity, and planning future growth.

Network monitoring encompasses several elements, including fault monitoring, performance monitoring, security monitoring, and account monitoring. Fault monitoring is about detecting and notifying problems. Performance monitoring looks at the quality of network services and ensures that everything is running optimally. Security monitoring focuses on detecting intrusion attempts and unauthorized activities. Account monitoring, on the other hand, tracks user activities, especially those related to access and authorization.

C++ is a powerful language that can significantly aid in network monitoring tasks. It provides low-level access to system and network resources, which means that it can retrieve the kind of detailed information that is often required in network monitoring. Its high performance makes it ideal for real-time monitoring applications that must process large amounts of network data quickly and efficiently. Libraries such as Boost.Asio can be used to create custom network monitoring tools, including packet sniffers, network scanners, and performance testers. In addition, the widespread use of C++ in network equipment means that many devices come with interfaces and APIs that can be accessed and manipulated using C++.

Fault Monitoring

Fault monitoring is a crucial part of network monitoring that focuses on identifying, alerting, and in some cases, rectifying faults within a network. This process is fundamental in maintaining the health and integrity of the network. Faults can stem from a variety of issues like device failures, connection losses, service disruptions, and many others. The primary goal is to detect these faults quickly so that corrective action can be taken before they escalate into more significant issues that could affect the entire network's performance or even cause a complete network outage.

Understanding Nagios

Nagios is a popular open-source network monitoring tool that is well-suited for fault monitoring. It provides complete monitoring of networks, servers, switches, applications, services, and other systems. Nagios can alert network administrators when devices go down, services fail, or when systems reach critical resource levels.

Nagios operates by using plugins, which are compiled executables or scripts that run on a schedule to check the status of a host or service. When a plugin's check command is executed, it determines the host or service's status and generates a result, which Nagios uses to take necessary actions based upon.

Install and Configure Nagios

Below is a step-by-step walkthrough on how to install and configure Nagios Core on Ubuntu. Please note that instructions may vary slightly for different Linux distributions:

Update System

First, update your system packages:

```
sudo apt-get update
sudo apt-get upgrade
```

Install Required Packages

Next, install the required packages:

```
sudo apt-get install build-essential libgd-dev openssl libssl-dev unzip apache2 php
libapache2-mod-php libperl-dev libltdl-dev wget
```

Create Nagios User and Group

Create a new user and group for Nagios:

```
sudo useradd nagios
sudo groupadd nagcmd
sudo usermod -a -G nagcmd nagios
```

Download and Extract Nagios Core

Download the latest version of Nagios Core and extract the files:

```
cd /tmp
wget
https://github.com/NagiosEnterprises/nagioscore/releases/download/nagios-
4.4.6/nagios-4.4.6.tar.gz
tar xzf nagios-4.4.6.tar.gz
cd nagios-4.4.6/
```

Compile and Install Nagios

Compile and install Nagios:

```
./configure --with-nagios-group=nagios --with-command-group=nagcmd --with-
httpd-conf=/etc/apache2/sites-enabled
make all
sudo make install
sudo make install-init
sudo make install-config
sudo make install-commandmode
```

Install Nagios Web Interface

Install the Nagios web interface:

```
sudo make install-webconf
```

Create User for Web Interface

Create a user for the web interface. You will be prompted to create a password for this user:

```
sudo htpasswd -c /usr/local/nagios/etc/htpasswd.users nagiosadmin
```

Configure Apache

Enable the Apache rewrite and cgi modules:

```
sudo a2enmod rewrite
sudo a2enmod cgi
```

Restart Apache

Restart the Apache service:

```
sudo systemctl restart apache2
```

Download and Install Nagios Plugins

Download and install Nagios plugins:

```
cd /tmp
wget https://nagios-plugins.org/download/nagios-plugins-2.3.3.tar.gz
tar xzf nagios-plugins-2.3.3.tar.gz
cd nagios-plugins-2.3.3/
./configure --with-nagios-user=nagios --with-nagios-group=nagios --with-openssl
make
sudo make install
```

Start Nagios

Add Nagios service to start on boot and start Nagios:

```
sudo systemctl enable nagios
sudo systemctl start nagios
```

After this, you should be able to access the Nagios web interface by opening a web browser and navigating to http://your_server_ip/nagios. Use the username nagiosadmin and the password you created in Step 7 to log in.

Remember to replace the URLs in the wget commands with the latest versions available on the official Nagios and Nagios Plugins websites.

Now, you can start adding hosts and services to your Nagios configuration for monitoring.

Monitor Hosts and Services on Nagios

After installing Nagios, you'll want to monitor hosts (computers, servers, routers, etc.) and services (HTTP, FTP, SSH, etc.) on your network. Below is how you can add hosts and services to your Nagios configuration:

Create Host and Service Definition Files

First, we need to create configuration files for our host and services. These will be placed in the /usr/local/nagios/etc/objects directory. Let us say we want to monitor a host named my-host.

Create a new configuration file:

```
sudo nano /usr/local/nagios/etc/objects/my-host.cfg
```

In this file, add the following to define your host:

```
define host{
    use                 linux-server
    host_name               my-host
    alias              My Host
    address              192.168.1.10
    }
```

Be sure to replace 192.168.1.10 with the actual IP address of your host.

Define Services to Monitor

In the same my-host.cfg file, we can define services that we want to monitor. For example, to monitor if the host is alive, and the SSH and HTTP services, add:

```
define service{
    use                 local-service
    host_name               my-host
    service_description    PING
```

```
    check_command        check_ping!100.0,20%!500.0,60%
    }

define service{
    use                  local-service
    host_name            my-host
    service_description  SSH
    check_command        check_ssh
    }

define service{
    use                  local-service
    host_name            my-host
    service_description  HTTP
    check_command        check_http
    }
```

Add Configuration File to Nagios

Now, we need to tell Nagios to use our new configuration file. Open the main Nagios configuration file:

```
sudo nano /usr/local/nagios/etc/nagios.cfg
```

Add the following line to the end of the file:

```
cfg_file=/usr/local/nagios/etc/objects/my-host.cfg
```

Verify and Restart Nagios

Before restarting Nagios, we should check our configuration files for any syntax errors. Use the following command:

```
sudo /usr/local/nagios/bin/nagios -v /usr/local/nagios/etc/nagios.cfg
```

If there are no errors, restart Nagios:

```
sudo systemctl restart nagios
```

Now, Nagios will start monitoring the host and services defined in your configuration file. You can view the status on the Nagios web interface.

we used check_ping, check_ssh, and check_http which are typically included with standard Nagios Plugins installation.

For other services or for monitoring network devices like switches and routers, you might need to install additional plugins or SNMP.

Using Nagios for Fault Monitoring

Below is a step-by-step walkthrough on how to setup Nagios for fault monitoring:

Installation

First, you need to install Nagios on a server. The installation process may vary depending on the operating system you are using. You can find detailed installation guides on the Nagios official website.

Configuration

Once installed, you need to configure Nagios to monitor your network. The main configuration file is nagios.cfg, located in the Nagios installation directory. This file defines where Nagios should look for object definition files, which contain configurations for hosts, services, contacts, and so on.

Define Hosts and Services

You need to define the hosts (devices, servers, etc.) and services (HTTP, FTP, SMTP, etc.) that you want Nagios to monitor. You do this by creating object definitions in the configuration files. Each host and service definition will include the check command that Nagios will execute to determine the status of that host or service.

Setting Alerts

Nagios allows you to set alerts that will notify you when a particular host or service goes down or behaves anomalously. Alerts can be sent via email, SMS, or any other method supported by the Nagios plugins you have installed.

Start Monitoring

After setting up hosts, services, and alerts, you can start the Nagios service. Nagios will begin checking the status of your defined hosts and services at the intervals you specified.

View Reports

Nagios provides a web interface where you can view current network status, notification history, problem history, log files, and other useful reports.

Maintenance

Regularly check your Nagios logs and keep your Nagios installation and plugins up to date to ensure smooth operation.

Nagios can be used with a C++ application and can be extended and controlled using scripts and compiled programs in a variety of languages, including C++, provided they adhere to the Nagios Plugin API.

Sample Program to Perform Fault Monitoring

Below is an example of how to use Nagios to perform fault monitoring.

In the previous step, you've already created a configuration file for your host and added it to the Nagios configuration. Let us assume you've added a host named my-host with the IP address 192.168.1.10, and you're monitoring the PING, SSH, and HTTP services on this host.

When Nagios starts monitoring, it will periodically check these services according to the check_interval specified in your service definitions. If it detects any anomalies such as a service is down or response time is beyond the acceptable range, it will raise an alert.

You can view these alerts through the Nagios web interface. To do this, open your web browser and go to http://<your-nagios-server>/nagios, then log in with your Nagios account.

Once logged in, you'll see the Nagios dashboard. Below are some key sections to pay attention to:

Service Status Details

This section gives detailed information about each service you're monitoring on all hosts. For each service, it shows its status (OK, Warning, Critical, or Unknown), last check time, status information, and a few more details.

For example, if the SSH service on my-host is down, you'll see its status as Critical and status information saying something like SSH CRITICAL - Socket timeout after 10 seconds.

Host Status Details

This section gives detailed information about each host you're monitoring. For each host, it shows its status (Up, Down, or Unreachable), last check time, status information, and a few more details.

If my-host is down, you'll see its status as Down and status information saying something like PING CRITICAL - Packet loss = 100%.

Problems

This section shows all current problems detected by Nagios. You can view all unhandled service problems, host problems, and all service or host problems, whether they're unhandled or acknowledged.

By default, Nagios sends alert notifications to contacts defined in your host or service definitions. So, in addition to checking the web interface, you also receive alert notifications via email or other methods you've configured. As you add more hosts and services to your Nagios configuration, you can monitor the entire network for faults and receive alerts to react promptly.

Performance Monitoring

Performance monitoring is the process of measuring and analyzing the operational characteristics of a system to understand its behavior, optimize its efficiency, and to detect and troubleshoot any performance-related issues. When applied to networking, performance monitoring encompasses tracking metrics like bandwidth usage, latency, packet loss, error rates, throughput, network device CPU utilization, and more. These metrics can give insights into how the network is performing and can help identify any bottlenecks or areas that might require improvement.

For instance, high latency could mean that data is taking too long to travel from one point in the network to another, which could negatively impact applications like voice and video conferencing that require real-time data transmission. On the other hand, high bandwidth usage might indicate that the network is nearing its capacity, potentially leading to network congestion and degraded performance. Performance monitoring can be done in real-time, where the metrics are tracked and analyzed continuously, or it can be done periodically at set intervals. The gathered data can be presented in various ways, such as in tables, charts, or graphs, to help visualize the performance trends and patterns.

Moreover, performance monitoring tools often come with alerting features that notify the administrators when certain thresholds are crossed. This helps in quickly identifying and resolving issues before they become critical and impact the business operations. When it comes to using C++ for network performance monitoring, there are libraries and APIs that allow for capturing network traffic, accessing network device statistics, and so on. A popular library is PCAP (or WinPCAP for Windows), which is used for capturing network packets.

The Boost ASIO library in C++ provides functionalities for asynchronous network programming, which can be leveraged to create efficient network performance monitoring applications. However, for comprehensive performance monitoring, especially in large and complex networks, full-fledged network monitoring solutions like Nagios are typically used offering extensive features for performance monitoring, alerting, visualization, and reporting, and they support a wide range of network devices and protocols.

Using Nagios for Performance Monitoring

Setting up performance monitoring with Nagios involves defining services that correspond to the performance metrics you want to monitor. Below is an example of how you might set up monitoring of the CPU load on a remote Linux host:

Install the Nagios Plugins on the Remote Linux Host

You'll need the check_nrpe and check_load plugins. These should be available in the Nagios plugins package which can be installed from the package manager of your Linux distribution.

Configure NRPE on the Remote Host

Open the NRPE configuration file (usually located at /etc/nagios/nrpe.cfg on the remote host, and add a command definition for checking the CPU load. It might look like this:

```
command[check_load]=/usr/lib/nagios/plugins/check_load -w 15,10,5 -c
30,25,20
```

This will set the warning levels for the load averages of the last 1, 5, and 15 minutes to 15, 10, and 5 respectively, and the critical levels to 30, 25, and 20.

Configure the Service in Nagios

On the Nagios server, open the configuration file where you have defined the hosts (usually located at /usr/local/nagios/etc/objects/hosts.cfg or similar), and add a service definition for checking the CPU load. It might look like this:

```
define service {
   use              generic-service
   host_name          remote_host
   service_description CPU Load
   check_command       check_nrpe!check_load
}
```

In the above sample program, remote_host should be replaced with the name of the host as defined in Nagios.

Verify and Reload Configuration

You should always verify your configuration files before reloading Nagios. This can be done using the nagios -v command, like this:

```
/usr/local/nagios/bin/nagios -v /usr/local/nagios/etc/nagios.cfg
```

If the verification process completes without errors, reload Nagios to apply the changes:

```
service nagios reload
```

Now Nagios will start monitoring the CPU load on the remote host, and it will send alerts according to the thresholds you defined. You can view the status of the service and any performance data collected in the Nagios web interface.

Security Monitoring

Security monitoring is a critical part of maintaining the integrity and safety of a network. It involves continuous surveillance of network activities to detect unusual behavior or unauthorized system access that might signal a security threat. This can range from detecting intrusions, malware or phishing attempts, to unauthorized data transfers or changes in system configurations.

There are several methods and tools for security monitoring:

- Intrusion Detection Systems (IDS): These systems actively monitor network traffic, looking for suspicious activities that might indicate an attack. IDS can be network-based (monitoring network traffic) or host-based (monitoring activities on a particular host).

- Intrusion Prevention Systems (IPS): These are similar to IDS but also have the ability to block potential threats, not just detect them.

- Firewall logs: Firewalls often have logging capabilities that record all traffic passing through them. These logs can be analyzed to identify potential threats or attacks.

- Security Information and Event Management (SIEM) Systems: These systems aggregate and analyze log data from a variety of network devices and servers. They can correlate events from different sources to help identify and mitigate potential threats.

- Vulnerability Scanners: These tools can be used to identify known vulnerabilities in your network infrastructure, such as outdated software versions, misconfigurations, or missing patches. Regularly scanning your network can help prevent security incidents.

For implementing security monitoring in C++, there are various libraries that can help with certain aspects of it, in addition to nagios, such as:

- Libpcap: It's a C/C++ library for network traffic capture, which can be used to build an IDS.

- OpenSSL: This is widely used for implementing secure communications, but can also be used to generate or verify digital signatures, or to encrypt log data for safe storage.

However, building a complete security monitoring solution from scratch can be a major undertaking. Many organizations use specialized security monitoring tools or services, some of which offer APIs or scripting capabilities that can be used to integrate them into your network management applications. It's important to understand that no single tool or method can guarantee complete security. Effective security monitoring requires a combination of tools and methods, along with a proactive approach to keeping up with the latest threats and vulnerabilities. A well-designed security monitoring system is an essential part of a defense-in-depth strategy, which involves multiple layers of security measures to protect your network.

Perform Security Monitoring using Nagios

Using Nagios for security monitoring involves a combination of using built-in Nagios services and adding custom plugins. Let us look at a simple scenario of monitoring an SSH server for security.

Install and Setup Nagios

Follow the steps described in the previous section to install Nagios Core and add hosts to monitor.

SSH Monitoring

To monitor an SSH server, add the following service definition in your Nagios configuration:

```
define service{
    use                     local-service
    host_name               your-host-name
    service_description     SSH
    check_command           check_ssh
    notifications_enabled   1
    }
```

This will instruct Nagios to periodically use its built-in check_ssh command to verify that the SSH server is up and running.

Monitoring Failed Login Attempts

Nagios doesn't provide built-in support for this kind of monitoring, but you can create a custom plugin. This plugin can, for example, check the system log for failed login attempts. For instance, you could create a shell script that counts the number of failed login attempts in the last 5 minutes:

```
#!/bin/bash

count=$(grep 'Failed password' /var/log/auth.log | awk -v d1="$(date --date="-5
```

```
min" "+%b %_d %H:%M")" -v d2="$(date "+%b %_d %H:%M")" '$0 > d1 &&
$0 < d2 || $0 ~ d2' | wc -l)

if [ "$count" -lt "5" ]; then
    echo "STATUS OK: $count failed SSH login attempts in the last 5 minutes."
    exit 0
elif [ "$count" -lt "10" ]; then
    echo "STATUS WARNING: $count failed SSH login attempts in the last 5
minutes."
    exit 1
else
    echo "STATUS CRITICAL: $count failed SSH login attempts in the last 5
minutes."
    exit 2
fi
```

This script counts the number of lines in the authentication log file that contain the phrase 'Failed password' and were written in the last 5 minutes. The script then returns an exit code and a message according to the Nagios plugin API specification, which allows Nagios to understand the result of the check.

Add the Custom Plugin to Nagios

Once you've created your custom plugin, you can add it to Nagios. Copy your script into the Nagios plugins directory, make it executable (chmod +x script.sh), then add a new command definition and a service definition to your Nagios configuration:

```
define command{
    command_name    check_failed_ssh
    command_line    /usr/local/nagios/libexec/check_failed_ssh.sh
    }

define service{
    use                 local-service
    host_name               your-host-name
```

```
service_description          SSH Failed Logins
check_command                check_failed_ssh
}
```

Apply Configuration Changes: Don't forget to verify your configuration files (nagios -v /usr/local/nagios/etc/nagios.cfg) and restart Nagios to apply the changes. Remember to adjust paths and parameters according to your specific setup or directory.

Account Monitoring

Account monitoring in the context of network monitoring typically involves keeping track of user activities and system access. This is crucial for maintaining the security of the system and ensuring that all users adhere to the proper use policies.

Below is an overview of what account monitoring might involve:

- User Activity Tracking: Monitor what users do on the system. This might include which files they access or modify, which commands they execute, and so forth. Many systems keep logs of user activities which can be monitored for suspicious behavior.

- System Access: Track who is logging into the system, when they log in, and from where. Unusual login times or locations might suggest that an account has been compromised.

- Privilege Usage: Monitor the use of system privileges. If a user suddenly starts performing administrative tasks that they usually don't do, this could be a sign of a problem.

- Account Changes: Keep track of changes to user accounts. This includes when accounts are created, modified, or deleted. Unauthorized changes could indicate a security breach.

As for monitoring these aspects in a practical way, we can consider Nagios for account monitoring. Monitoring these aspects with Nagios will involve the use of NRPE (Nagios Remote Plugin Executor) or similar tools, along with custom scripts that can check the aspects mentioned above. NRPE allows you to remotely execute Nagios plugins on other Linux/Unix machines. This allows you to monitor remote machine metrics (disk usage, CPU load, etc.). While Nagios does have built-in support for some aspects of system monitoring (like disk usage, CPU usage, etc.), it does not have built-in support for specific account monitoring tasks for which you have to write custom scripts that perform the desired checks and can be called as Nagios plugins.

For instance, you can write a bash script that checks the number of failed login attempts for a particular user, or checks for any changes to the /etc/passwd file where user account information is typically stored. This script can then be set up as a Nagios plugin, so that Nagios can call the script and interpret its output.

Perform Account Monitoring with Custom Nagios Plugin

While Nagios doesn't have built-in support for specific account monitoring tasks, you can write a custom script that checks for account-related activities and use it as a Nagios plugin. Below is an example on how you can create a simple plugin to monitor SSH log-in attempts:

Create the Plugin Script

First, create a bash script that will read the log file for SSH log-ins. In many systems, these logs can be found in /var/log/auth.log. Below is a simple example of what that script might look like:

```
#!/bin/bash

# The location of the auth.log file
AUTH_LOG=/var/log/auth.log

# Count the number of successful SSH log-ins in the last day
SUCCESS_COUNT=$(grep -i "Accepted password" $AUTH_LOG | grep
"$(date '+%b %e')" | wc -l)

# Count the number of failed SSH log-ins in the last day
FAIL_COUNT=$(grep -i "Failed password" $AUTH_LOG | grep "$(date '+%b
%e')" | wc -l)

echo "SSH Log-ins: $SUCCESS_COUNT successful, $FAIL_COUNT failed"
```

Set up the Script as a Nagios Plugin

To use this script as a Nagios plugin, you first need to move it to the directory where Nagios keeps its plugins, usually /usr/lib/nagios/plugins. You should also make sure the script is executable by running:

```
chmod +x script_name.sh.
```

Configure Nagios to Use the Plugin

Finally, you need to configure Nagios to use your new plugin. In your Nagios configuration file (usually /etc/nagios/nagios.cfg), add a new command definition for your plugin:

```
define command {
   command_name check_ssh_logins
   command_line /usr/lib/nagios/plugins/check_ssh_logins.sh
}
```

Then, in the host or service configuration where you want to use the plugin, reference the new command:

```
define service {
   use generic-service
   host_name my_host
   service_description SSH Login Monitor
   check_command check_ssh_logins
}
```

After reloading the Nagios configuration, Nagios should start using your new plugin to monitor SSH log-ins.

Summary

Network Monitoring is a crucial part of network administration as it allows for the identification and resolution of issues before they impact users or cause downtime. The chapter commenced by stressing the importance of network monitoring and its various elements, including fault, performance, security, and account monitoring, all achievable through C++. The fault monitoring section emphasized detecting and diagnosing problems in the network infrastructure. We explored Nagios, a powerful open-source tool used widely for fault monitoring. Detailed steps for installing and configuring Nagios on Linux were provided, including how to add hosts and services to the Nagios configuration for monitoring. Practical demonstrations showcased how to create plugins for Nagios to monitor specific aspects of a system.

Performance monitoring focused on ensuring the network is performing optimally, and Nagios's role was elaborated in this regard. Similarly, we touched upon security monitoring, an integral part of any network administration task to protect network resources from unauthorized access or attacks. We demonstrated using Nagios for security monitoring tasks. Lastly, the account monitoring section explored the monitoring of user accounts, especially for activities like SSH log-in attempts. A custom script was used as a Nagios plugin to illustrate how account monitoring could be done.

This chapter serves as an essential guide to network monitoring, highlighting its importance and demonstrating how to effectively use a tool like Nagios in a variety of monitoring scenarios. The practical examples using C++ and Nagios provide a strong foundation for implementing and customizing network monitoring to suit unique network environments.

CHAPTER 11: NETWORK TROUBLESHOOTING

Beginning with Network Troubleshooting

Network troubleshooting is an inevitable part of any network administrator's responsibilities. It involves identifying, diagnosing, and resolving problems and issues within a computer network. Having a structured approach to network troubleshooting can make the process more efficient and effective.

The general troubleshooting methodology that most network administrators follow typically involves several steps: defining the problem, identifying the scope of the problem, identifying the possible causes, identifying the actual cause, implementing a solution, and finally, verifying the solution. This systematic approach helps in isolating the issue and addressing it more effectively.

Various tools are available to help in the troubleshooting process. The 'ping' command is one of the most basic yet powerful tools to test the connectivity between two network nodes. 'Traceroute' or 'tracert' is another utility for displaying the path that packets take to reach a network host, helping identify where a packet gets lost or delayed. 'Nslookup' is a tool used for querying the DNS servers and troubleshooting DNS related issues. 'Netstat' is a versatile command-line tool that displays network statistics and ongoing network connections, proving useful for spotting unusual connections or services.

In terms of packet sniffers, 'Wireshark' is a well-known, widely-used network protocol analyzer. It lets you see what's happening on your network at a microscopic level, and is the de facto standard across many commercial and non-profit enterprises. 'TCPdump' is another powerful command-line packet analyzer; it allows the user to display TCP/IP and other packets being transmitted or received over a network to which the computer is attached.

In essence, network troubleshooting is a systematic process that, aided by various command-line tools and packet sniffers, allows network administrators to diagnose and address issues in a network. A solid understanding of these tools and their utility is a key skill in managing and maintaining a robust and efficient network.

Network Troubleshooting Methodology

Network troubleshooting methodology involves a structured approach to identifying and resolving network issues. It requires careful analysis, proposed solutions, rigorous testing, and detailed documentation, which collectively helps maintain the health and efficiency of the network.

Let us delve into each step of the Network Troubleshooting Methodology:

Identify

The first step of network troubleshooting is to identify the problem. This is typically done by gathering information from end users or system alerts. A network admin needs to determine what the problem is, when it started, and how it's affecting the network. For example, users might report that they are unable to access a certain service, or an automated alert might indicate high latency or packet loss on a particular network segment.

Diagnose

Once the problem has been identified, the next step is to diagnose the issue. This involves identifying the root cause of the problem. Network administrators use a variety of tools for this, such as ping, traceroute, and packet sniffers like Wireshark. In our example, the network admin might find that a router is down, or that a software bug is causing the service to fail.

Propose

After diagnosing the issue, the network admin will propose a solution. This solution should directly address the root cause identified in the previous step. For example, if the issue was a failing router, the proposed solution might be to replace the router. If a software bug was the issue, the solution might be to apply a patch or update.

Test

After the solution has been proposed, it needs to be tested. This is an important step to make sure that the solution actually resolves the issue and doesn't introduce new problems. The testing phase might involve deploying the new router in a test environment before the live network, or applying the software patch to a test system before updating the production server.

Document

Once the solution has been successfully tested and implemented, it's essential to document the issue, the steps taken to resolve it, and the final outcome. This helps to build a knowledge base for reference in case similar issues arise in the future. This documentation might include the initial user reports, the troubleshooting steps undertaken, the proposed and implemented solution, and any changes observed after the solution was implemented.

Using Ping

Ping is a simple yet powerful command-line tool used to test the reachability of a host on an Internet Protocol (IP) network. It measures the round-trip time for messages sent from the originating host to a destination computer. It operates by sending Internet Control Message Protocol (ICMP) Echo Request messages and waiting for Echo Replies.

Below is a detailed look at the command:

To use ping, simply open your command line interface (on Windows, this is usually Command Prompt; on Linux or Mac, this is Terminal) and type ping followed by the IP address or the domain name of the host you wish to test, e.g., ping google.com or ping 8.8.8.8.

Ping will send a series of packets to the target host and receive responses. For each response received, ping will display the results - how long each packet took to make the round-trip.

By default, the ping command will continue to send packets indefinitely until you stop it. To stop the ping command, press Ctrl + C.

Now, let us go through a few practical examples:

Example 1: Basic Ping

In your terminal, type ping www.google.com. This will start sending ICMP Echo Request packets to Google's server. Each line returned will show you the time it took for the packet to reach Google's server and come back.

Example 2: Limit Number of Ping Requests

By default, ping will keep pinging the host until you stop it. But you can limit the number of requests. On Linux or macOS, use the -c (count) option. On Windows, use -n.

For instance, to send exactly 5 ping requests to Google's server, you would use:

On Linux/macOS:

```
ping -c 5 www.google.com
```

On Windows:

```
ping -n 5 www.google.com
```

Example 3: Increasing the Timeout

You can also increase the timeout period (the time that ping waits for a reply before giving up) with the -W option on Linux/macOS or -w on Windows. The timeout value is in seconds.

On Linux/macOS:

```
ping -c 3 -W 10 www.google.com (wait for up to 10 seconds for a reply)
```

On Windows:

```
ping -n 3 -w 10000 www.google.com (wait for up to 10000 milliseconds, or 10 seconds, for a reply)
```

The ping command is a versatile tool and the above examples just scratch the surface of what it's capable of. Many other options are available and you can explore them by typing ping --help (on Linux/macOS) or ping /? (on Windows) to see a full list.

Using Tracert/Traceroute

The tracert command (known as traceroute on Linux and macOS) is a command-line tool used to track and display the route that a packet takes to reach a destination on a network. It displays the series of IP addresses that the packet travels through to reach the destination. This tool is especially useful for troubleshooting network issues, as it can help to identify where along the path the problem occurs.

Below is how it works in detail:

To use tracert or traceroute, open your command line interface and type tracert (on Windows) or traceroute (on Linux or macOS), followed by the IP address or domain name of the destination host. For example, tracert www.google.com or traceroute www.google.com.

The tool will then send packets towards the destination and list each router or hop along the way. Each line represents one hop, and it displays the IP address (and often the domain name) of the router at that hop.

Now, let us look at a few examples:

Example 1: Basic Traceroute

In your terminal, type tracert www.google.com (on Windows) or traceroute www.google.com (on Linux or macOS). This will begin tracing the route that packets take from your machine to Google's server. Each line represents a hop along the route.

Example 2: Specifying the Number of Hops

Sometimes, you might want to limit the number of hops that traceroute will attempt before giving up. To do this, you can use the -h option followed by the maximum number of hops. For instance:

On Linux/macOS:

```
traceroute -m 5 www.google.com (trace the route to Google's server, but give up after 5 hops)
```

On Windows, you would use the -h option like this:

```
tracert -h 5 www.google.com.
```

Example 3: Using ICMP instead of UDP

By default, traceroute uses UDP datagrams on Unix-like systems. However, you can use ICMP Echo Request messages (like those used by the ping command) instead with the -I option. This can be useful in networks where UDP is blocked. Below is an example:

On Linux/macOS:

```
traceroute -I www.google.com
```

Remember that the full set of options and how they're used can vary between systems, so it's always a good idea to check the manual page for traceroute on your system by typing man traceroute (on Linux/macOS) or tracert /? (on Windows) in your terminal.

Using Nslookup

The nslookup command is a network administration tool for querying the Domain Name System (DNS) to obtain domain name or IP address mappings, or any other specific DNS records. It stands for 'name server lookup'. This tool can be used from a command line interface, and is available on most networked computer systems.

Below is how it works in detail:

To use nslookup, open your command line interface and type nslookup, followed by the domain name or IP address you want to query. For example, nslookup www.google.com.

The tool will then return the domain name or IP address associated with that domain name, as well as the name server that provided the information.

Now, let us look at a few examples:

Example 1: Basic Nslookup

In your terminal, type nslookup www.google.com. This will return the IP address associated with Google's server, as well as the name server that provided the information.

Example 2: Reverse DNS Lookup

You can use nslookup to perform a reverse DNS lookup, which means you start with an IP address and find its associated domain name. To do this, you would type nslookup, followed by the IP address. For example, nslookup 8.8.8.8. This will return the domain name associated with that IP address.

Example 3: Querying Specific DNS Record Type

You can use nslookup to query for a specific DNS record type. For instance, to get the mail server (MX record) for a domain, you would type nslookup -query=mx, followed by the domain name. For example, nslookup -query=mx google.com. This will return the mail server for the google.com domain.

Using Netstat

The netstat command (network statistics) is a command-line tool that displays network connections (both incoming and outgoing), routing tables, and a number of network interface and network protocol statistics. It is useful for checking your network's overall health, to find out how well your firewall is working, and for spotting suspicious network activity.

To use netstat, you open your command line interface and type netstat, possibly followed by some options. By default, it shows a list of active sockets for each protocol it supports. Now, let us look at a few examples:

Example 1: Basic Netstat

In your terminal, type netstat. This will list all current network connections, along with protocol used, local and foreign addresses, and the state of the connection.

Example 2: Displaying Only Listening Sockets

You can use netstat to display only sockets that are listening for incoming connections. To do this, you would type netstat -l. This is useful to quickly check what services are waiting for connections on your machine.

Example 3: Displaying Statistics

Netstat can also display statistics for each network protocol. To do this, you would type netstat -s. This will print detailed statistics for each protocol, like the number of packets received, transmitted, discarded, etc.

Example 4: Continuously Display Network Status

To make netstat continuously refresh network status, you can use the c option like netstat -c. This will refresh the information every second, allowing you to monitor real-time changes to your network.

Exploring Wireshark

About Wireshark

Wireshark is a potent, open-source tool that enables deep inspection of network traffic, making it invaluable for network troubleshooting and protocol analysis. Its functionality encompasses various areas, such as software and communications protocol development, effectively serving as a diagnostic microscope for network health. Wireshark captures and displays data packets transmitted within a network, thereby offering a granular view of traffic details. This detailed insight makes it possible to identify anomalies, bottlenecks, and potential security threats in real-time. Furthermore, it can decode and analyze data from different network protocols, providing a versatile tool for IT professionals, network administrators, and developers to optimize and secure their networks.

Features

Wireshark has several features that make it a powerful tool for network analysis:

- Deep inspection of hundreds of protocols.
- Live capture and offline analysis.
- Ability to read/write many different capture file formats.
- Filtering and coloring rules can be applied for more effective analysis.
- Rich VoIP (Voice over IP) analysis.

Installation of Wireshark

Begin by updating your system's package list using the following command:

```
sudo apt update
```

After updating the system, install Wireshark using the command:

```
sudo apt install wireshark
```

During the installation, a popup window will appear asking whether non-superusers should be able to capture packets. Choose 'Yes' if you want to allow this.

After the installation process completes, you can verify it by typing:

```
wireshark --version
```

This will display the version of Wireshark that you installed.

Wireshark Configuration

Start Wireshark from the terminal by just typing wireshark and pressing enter. Alternatively, it should also appear in your system's application menu.

When Wireshark opens, you will see a list of the network interfaces on your system. Click the name of the interface that you want to capture data from. This will start the capture process.

You can filter the traffic using the 'Apply a display filter' field. For example, typing http will only display HTTP traffic.

Click the stop button to stop capturing traffic. Now you can analyze the traffic in detail.

Exploring Tcpdump

About Tcpdump

Tcpdump is a versatile command-line packet analyzer tool prevalent in Unix and Linux distributions. Essentially, it's a network monitoring tool that allows users to capture or "sniff" TCP/IP packets and other types of data packets in real-time, flowing in and out of network interfaces. By capturing these packets, users can diagnose network issues, analyze network performance, or scrutinize the data traffic on a network. Its command-line interface ensures a lightweight footprint, making it an efficient and powerful tool for network analysis and troubleshooting, whether it's for understanding network protocols, crafting security policies, or investigating network anomalies.

Features

- Versatile: tcpdump can capture or "sniff" traffic on any network to which the computer is attached.
- Expressive: Its filtering capability allows users to zero in on traffic based on specific criteria.
- Portable: As a command-line tool, it can be used on virtually any Unix/Linux system.
- Detailed: It provides detailed information about packet structure and protocol.
- Scriptable: As a command-line tool, its output can be easily redirected, processed, and analyzed with scripts.

Installation of Tcpdump

If your system doesn't have tcpdump installed, you can install it using the package manager of your Linux distribution. Below are instructions for Debian-based systems:

Update your system's package list using the command:

```
sudo apt update
```

Install tcpdump using the command:

```
sudo apt install tcpdump
```

Verify the installation by checking the version of tcpdump:

```
tcpdump --version
```

While using tcpdump, it typically requires root privileges. Below are some simplified demonstrations of how you can use it:

Examples

Capture packets from a specific interface:

```
sudo tcpdump -i eth0
```

Replace eth0 with the interface you want to monitor.

Capture and save packets to a file:

```
sudo tcpdump -i eth0 -w filename.pcap
```

This command saves the packets to filename.pcap.

Read from a saved packet file:

```
tcpdump -r filename.pcap
```

This command reads packets from filename.pcap.

Capture ICMP packets using a filter:

```
sudo tcpdump icmp
```

Summary

In this Chapter, we deeply delved into the vital area of network troubleshooting. We started by understanding the network troubleshooting methodology, a systematic approach often used by network administrators to identify, diagnose, propose solutions, test, and document network problems. This methodology is crucial to avoid recurrent issues and maintain a reliable network infrastructure.

Next, we explored essential network troubleshooting tools, beginning with 'ping', a simple yet effective tool used to verify network host reachability and network latency. We then covered 'tracert' (trace route), a powerful command-line tool used to track the path that a packet takes from the source system to the destination system. Moving on, we discussed 'nslookup', a command-line tool used for querying the DNS (Domain Name System) to obtain domain name or IP address mapping, and other DNS records. We also went through 'netstat', a versatile tool that provides information and statistics about protocols in use and current TCP/IP network connections.

Finally, we studied packet sniffers like Wireshark and tcpdump. Wireshark, a popular GUI-based network protocol analyzer, enables users to see what's happening on their network at a microscopic level. We learnt how to install, configure, and capture network packets using Wireshark. On the other hand, tcpdump, a command-line packet sniffer, came next. It's a powerful tool used for network debugging and troubleshooting. We walked through its features, installation, and some practical examples of its usage. By the end of this chapter, we had a robust understanding of a variety of tools and methodologies for network troubleshooting, crucial for any network administrator or anyone working in the network management and operation domain.

Thank You

Index

8

802.11 standards 83, 91

A

Accepting Connections 23
Access Control Lists 146, 148
Account Monitoring 164, 165
Application Layer 43, 44, 60, 78
async/await 95, 97, 98, 111
Asynchronous I/O .... i, 104, 105
Asynchronous Programming 7, 93, 94

B

Bluetooth 75, 77, 78, 79, 80, 83, 84, 91
Bluetooth Programming 79
Bluetooth protocol 79
Boost Asio 49, 61
Boost.Asio 2, 7, 10, 12, 23, 26, 29, 37, 41, 42, 47, 59, 61, 85, 94, 98, 100, 103, 105, 115, 120, 121, 134, 150

C

Callbacks 95, 98, 111
Concurrency 101, 112

D

Diagnostic Tools 145
distribution ii
DNS19, 21, 26, 34, 44, 46, 47, 57, 58, 61, 104, 134, 169, 174, 179
DNS Queries 58
Domain Name System (DNS) 57, 174

E

Encryption 86
Error Handling 29, 59, 89

F

Fault Monitoring 150, 156, 157
Firewalls 146, 161
Firmware Updates 139, 140
FTP 8, 21, 44, 45, 52, 53, 61, 140, 141, 154, 156
Functional Testing 114, 115, 117, 132

H

HTTP 8, 15, 21, 44, 45, 47, 49, 51, 61, 154, 155, 156, 157, 177
HTTP protocol 44
HTTPS request 47, 49, 61

I

IKEv2 .... 66, 67
IMAP protocol 46, 57
IP addresses ... 33, 34, 35, 36, 37, 41, 42, 46, 57, 59, 61, 125, 129, 131, 132, 134, 138, 172
IPsec 64, 66, 67

L

L2TP 64, 66, 67
libuv 104, 105, 109, 112

M

Multithreading 7, 8, 101, 112

N

Nagios 151, 152, 153, 154, 155, 156, 157, 158, 159, 160, 162, 163, 164, 165, 166, 167
Nagios Core 151, 152, 162
Nagios Plugins 153, 156, 159
NETCONF 135, 136, 137, 138, 139, 147
NETCONF protocol 138
netstat 174, 175, 179
Network Byte Order 30
Network Configuration 133, 134, 135, 138, 139, 147
Network Configuration Management 133, 134,

147
Network Monitoring 149, 150, 166
Network Protocols 8
Network Simulation 124, 125, 128, 129
Network Simulations 124, 125
Network Testing 113, 114
Network Testing Methodologies 114
Network Troubleshooting 168, 169
Network Troubleshooting Methodology 169
NS-3 114, 125, 126, 127, 128, 129, 130, 132
nslookup 174, 179

O

OpenVPN 64, 66, 67, 68, 69, 70, 71, 72, 73
OpenVPN Configuration 68

P

Packet loss 158
Performance Monitoring 158, 159
Performance Testing 115, 118, 120, 132
Ping 171
Port Numbers 16, 18
PPTP 64, 66, 67
prior ii
Promises 95, 96, 111

R

Remote Access VPN 65, 66, 70, 72

S

Secure Sockets Layer (SSL) 45, 66
Security Monitoring 160, 162
Server Socket 23, 26
Site-to-Site VPN 65, 69, 72
SMTP 8, 15, 21, 44, 46, 54, 55, 56, 57, 61, 156
Socket Programming 22, 29, 59
SSL/TLS 49, 51, 67
SSL/TLS handshake 49, 51
Synchronous Programming 94

T

Task 135
TCP/IP 15, 16, 18, 44, 127, 139, 169, 177, 179
TCP/IP model 44
tcpdump 177, 178, 179
Thread 104
Traceroute 169, 172, 173
Tracert 172
Transport Layer 45, 47, 66
Transport Layer Security (TLS) 45, 66

U

UDP 14, 15, 18, 19, 20, 21, 22, 23, 26, 28, 29, 30, 31, 40, 42, 44, 57, 61, 67, 104, 127, 128, 131, 139, 142, 143, 148, 173

V

VPN 63, 64, 65, 66, 67, 68, 69, 70, 71, 72, 73
VPN Client 63
VPN Protocols 66, 67
VPN Tunnel 63

W

WEP 75, 85, 86, 91
WiFi 75, 76, 77, 91, 127
Wireless Networks 74, 75, 88
Wireless Security Standards 85
Wireless Standards 83
Wireshark 128, 169, 170, 175, 176, 179
WPA 75, 86, 88, 89, 91
WPA2 75, 76, 85, 86, 87, 91
WPA3 75, 76, 85, 86, 87, 91

Z

Zigbee 81, 83, 91

Epilogue

Now that we have reached the end of our journey with "C++ Networking 101," it is time to take stock of the journey that we have taken. We began with the fundamentals of C++ and networking libraries and worked our way up the hierarchical structure of knowledge and capabilities step by step. We have covered a vast expanse of network administration, from an understanding of TCP and UDP, IP configuration, routing and switching, to securing networks, managing wireless networks, DNS management, troubleshooting, and finally automating network operations.

Real-world examples and case studies helped to bring the theory to life and provided useful insights into the day-to-day responsibilities of network administrators. We learned our way around the C++ world and discovered how its power can be put to use in various networking-related activities. Nevertheless, this is not the end of our journey. The terrain of network administration is always shifting and becoming more complex. The development of new technologies has resulted in the emergence of both new challenges and new opportunities. In order to become successful future network administrators, you will need to maintain a flexible mindset and continually improve your professional abilities in order to keep up with emerging industry standards and cutting-edge technology.

The purpose of the course "C++ Networking 101" was not simply to instruct you in network administration; rather, it was to instil in you a mentality that is open to learning, which is adaptable, and which is innovative. Your career in network administration should have a solid foundation, and the knowledge and skills you acquire through reading this book should serve as a solid foundation for that foundation. When you are ready to apply what you have learned in the classroom to the real world, keep in mind that the essential qualities of a good network administrator include not only their technical expertise but also their problem-solving skills, their adaptability, and their willingness to advance along with the changing digital landscape.

I hope that all of your future endeavours are successful for you. Always keep in mind that the digital universe is waiting for your expertise. Assume the role of the driving force behind efficient and safe digital communication.

Made in the USA
Monee, IL
07 July 2026